PETER PLYMLEY'S LETTERS AND SELECTED ESSAYS

BY

SYDNEY SMITH

British Library Cataloguing-in-Publication Data
A catalogue record for this book is available from the
British Library

Contents

Sydney Smith

Sydney Smith was born on 3rd June 1771 in Woodford, Essex, England.

Smith was educated at Winchester College, where he greatly distinguished himself, rising to the position of school captain. In fact, he and his brother were so recognised for thier all-round abilities that their school fellows signed a round-robin "refusing to try for the college prizes if the Smiths were allowed to contend for them anymore".

In 1789, upon leaving Winchester College, he became a scholar at New College, Oxford. He received a fellowship from the college and finally obtained his Master of Arts degree in 1796. Smith's intention was to go on to read for the bar, but his father refused and compelled him to join the clergy. He was ordained at Oxford in 1796 and became the curate of the village of Netheravon, near Amesbury in Salisbury Plain. The squire of the parish engaged Smith to tutor his son and the pair went to Edinburgh to study. While his pupil attended lectures, Smith studied moral philosophy, medicine, and chemistry.

Smith's first book 'Six Sermons, preached in Charlotte Street Chapel, Edinburgh' was published in 1800. He married Catharine Amelia Pybus in the same year and the couple settled in Edinburgh. While there, he helped set up the *Edinburgh Review* and became its first editor in 1802. He continued to write articles for the review for the next quarter of the century which were a key element to the publication's success.

Smith left Scotland in 1803 and relocated to London. He became well known as a preacher, lecturer, and society figure, and he often preached to huge crowds in Berkeley Chapel, Mayfair.. He lectured at the Royal Institution on moral philosophy and promoted progressive values such as the education of women and the abolition of slavery. He often destroyed paper copies of his lectures after they had served their purpose but his wife rescued some of the charred manuscripts and published them as 'Elementary Sketches of Moral Philosophy' in 1850.

His most famous work is *Peter Plymley's Letters* (1892) in which he deals with the subject of Catholic emancipation, ridiculing the opposition of the country clergy.

Smith continued his career in the church, preaching in Yorkshire for twenty years and being appointed to a residentiary canonry at St Paul's Cathedral in 1831.

He is remembered as a fine wit and humourist, and is often quoted in English literary life. Smith died on 22nd February 1845.

INTRODUCTION.

Sydney Smith, of the same age as Walter Scott, was born at Woodford, in Essex, in the year 1771, and he died of heart disease, aged seventy-four, on the 22nd of February, 1845. His father was a clever man of wandering habits who, when he settled in England, reduced his means by buying, altering, spoiling, and then selling about nineteen different places in England. His mother was of a French family from Languedoc, that had been driven to England by the Revocation of the Edict of Nantes. Sydney Smith's grandfather, upon the mother's side, could speak no English, and he himself ascribed some of his gaiety to the French blood in his veins.

He was one of four sons. His eldest brother Robert— known as Bobus--was sent to Eton, where he joined Canning, Frere, and John Smith, in writing the Eton magazine, the Microcosm; and at Cambridge Bobus afterwards was known as a fine Latin scholar. Sydney Smith went first to a school at Southampton, and then to Winchester, where he became captain of the school. Then he was sent for six months to Normandy for a last polish to his French before he went on to New College, Oxford. When he had obtained his fellowship there, his father left him to his own resources. His eldest brother had been trained for the bar, his two younger brothers were sent out to India, and Sydney, against his own wish, yielded to the strong desire of his father that he should take orders as a clergyman. Accordingly, in 1794, he became curate of the small parish of Netherhaven, in Wiltshire. Meat came to Netherhaven only once a week in a butcher's cart from Salisbury, and the curate often dined upon potatoes flavoured with ketchup.

The only educated neighbour was Mr. Hicks Beach, the squire, who at first formally invited the curate to dinner on Sundays, and soon found his wit, sense, and high culture so delightful, that the acquaintance ripened into friendship. After two years in the curacy, Sydney Smith gave it up and went abroad with the squire's son. "When first I went into the Church," he wrote afterwards, "I had a curacy in the middle of Salisbury Plain; the parish was Netherhaven, near Amesbury. The squire of the parish, Mr. Beach, took a fancy to me, and after I had served it two years, he engaged me as tutor to his eldest son, and it was arranged that I and his son should proceed to the University of Weimar in Saxony. We set out, but before reaching our destination Germany was disturbed by war, and, in stress of politics, we put into Edinburgh, where I remained five years."

Young Michael Beach, who had little taste for study, lived with Sydney Smith as his tutor, and found him a wise guide and pleasant friend. When Michael went to the University, his brother William was placed under the same good care. Sydney Smith, about the same time, went to London to be married. His wife's rich brother quarrelled with her for marrying a man who said that his only fortune consisted in six small silver teaspoons. One day after their happy marriage he ran in to his wife and threw them in her lap, saying, "There, Kate, you lucky girl, I give you all my fortune!" The lucky girl had a small fortune of her own which her husband had strictly secured to herself and her children. Mr. Beach recognised the value of Sydney Smith's influence over his son by a wedding gift of 750 pounds. In 1802 a daughter was born, and in the same year Sydney Smith joined Francis Jeffrey and other friends, who then maintained credit for Edinburgh as the Modern Athens, in the founding of The Edinburgh Review, to which the papers in this volume, added to the Peter Plymley Letters, were contributed. The Rev. Sydney Smith preached sometimes in the Episcopal Church at Edinburgh, and presently had, in addition to William Beach, a son of Mr. Gordon, of Ellon Castle, placed under his care, receiving 400 pounds a year for each of the young men.

In 1803 Sydney Smith left Edinburgh for London, where he wrote busily in The Edinburgh Review, but remained poor for many years. His wit brought friends, and the marriage of his eldest brother with Lord Holland's aunt quickened the growth of a strong friendship with Lord Holland.

Through the good offices of Lord Holland, Sydney Smith obtained, in 1806, aged thirty-five, the living of Foston-le-Clay, in Yorkshire. In the next year appeared the first letter of Peter Plymley to his brother Abraham on the subject of the Irish Catholics.

These letters fell, we are told, like sparks on a heap of gunpowder. All London, and soon all England, was alive to the sound reason recommended by a lively wit. Sydney Smith lived to be recognised as first among the social wits, and it was always the chief praise of his wit that wisdom was the soul of it. Peter Plymley's letters, and Sydney Smith's articles on the same subject in The Edinburgh Review were the most powerful aids furnished by the pen to the solution of the burning question of their time. Lord Murray called the Plymley letters "after Pascal's letters the most instructive piece of wisdom in the form of irony ever written." Worldly wealth came later; but in wit, wisdom, and kindly helpful cheerfulness, from youth to age, Sydney Smith's life was rich.

H. M.

LETTERS ON THE SUBJECT OF THE CATHOLICS.

TO MY BROTHER ABRAHAM, WHO LIVES IN THE COUNTRY.
BY PETER PLYMLEY.

LETTER I.

Dear Abraham,—A worthier and better man than yourself does not exist; but I have always told you, from the time of our boyhood, that you were a bit of a goose. Your parochial affairs are governed with exemplary order and regularity; you are as powerful in the vestry as Mr. Perceval is in the House of Commons,—and, I must say, with much more reason; nor do I know any church where the faces and smock-frocks of the congregation are so clean, or their eyes so uniformly directed to the preacher. There is another point, upon which I will do you ample justice; and that is, that the eyes so directed towards you are wide open; for the rustic has, in general, good principles, though he cannot control his animal habits; and, however loud he may snore, his face is perpetually turned towards the fountain of orthodoxy.

Having done you this act of justice, I shall proceed, according to our ancient intimacy and familiarity, to explain to you my opinions about the Catholics, and to reply to yours.

In the first place, my sweet Abraham, the Pope is not landed—nor are there any curates sent out after him—nor has he been hid at St. Albans by the Dowager Lady Spencer—nor dined privately at Holland House—nor been seen near Dropmore. If these fears exist (which I do not believe), they exist only in the mind of the Chancellor of the Exchequer; they emanate from his zeal for the Protestant interest; and, though they reflect the highest honour upon the delicate irritability of his faith, must certainly be considered as more ambiguous proofs of the sanity and vigour of his understanding. By this time, however, the best-informed clergy in the neighbourhood of the metropolis are convinced that the rumour is without foundation; and though the Pope is probably hovering about our coast in a fishing-smack, it is most likely he will fall a prey to the vigilance of our cruisers; and it is certain that he has not yet polluted the Protestantism of our soil.

Exactly in the same manner, the story of the wooden gods seized at Charing Cross, by an order from the Foreign Office, turns out to be without the shadow of a foundation; instead of the angels and archangels, mentioned by the informer, nothing was discovered but a wooden image of Lord Mulgrave, going down to Chatham, as a head- piece for the Spanker gun-vessel; it was an exact resemblance of his Lordship in his military uniform; and THEREFORE as little like a god as can well be imagined.

Having set your fears at rest, as to the extent of the conspiracy formed against the Protestant religion, I will now come to the argument itself.

You say these men interpret the scriptures in an unorthodox manner, and that they eat their god.—Very likely. All this may seem very important to you, who live fourteen miles from a market-town, and, from long residence upon your living, are become a kind of holy vegetable; and in a theological sense it is highly important. But I want soldiers and sailors for the state; I want to make a greater use than I now can do of a poor country full of men; I want to render the military service popular among the Irish; to check the power of France; to make every possible exertion for the safety of Europe, which in twenty years' time will be nothing but a mass of French slaves: and then you, and ten other such boobies as you, call out—"For God's sake, do not think of raising cavalry and infantry in Ireland! . . . They interpret the Epistle to Timothy in a different manner from what we do! . . . They eat a bit of wafer every Sunday, which they call their God!" . . . I wish to my soul they would eat you, and such reasoners as you are. What! when Turk, Jew, Heretic, Infidel, Catholic, Protestant, are all combined against this country; when men of every religious persuasion, and no religious persuasion; when the population of half the globe is up in arms against us; are we to stand examining our generals and armies as a bishop examines a candidate for holy orders; and to suffer no one to bleed for England who does not agree with you about the second of Timothy? You talk about the Catholics! If you and your brotherhood have been able to persuade the country into a continuation of this grossest of all absurdities, you have ten times the power which the Catholic clergy ever had in their best days. Louis XIV., when he revoked the Edict of Nantes, never thought of preventing the Protestants from fighting his battles; and gained accordingly some of his most splendid victories by the talents of his Protestant generals. No power in Europe, but yourselves, has ever thought for these hundred years past, of asking whether a bayonet is Catholic, or Presbyterian or Lutheran; but whether it is sharp and well-tempered. A bigot delights in public ridicule; for he begins to think he is a martyr. I can promise you the full enjoyment of this pleasure, from one extremity of Europe to the other.

I am as disgusted with the nonsense of the Roman Catholic religion as you can be: and no man who talks such nonsense shall ever tithe the product of the earth, nor meddle with the ecclesiastical establishment in any shape; but what have I to do with the speculative nonsense of his theology, when the object is to elect the mayor of a county town, or to appoint a colonel of a marching regiment? Will a man discharge the solemn impertinences of the one office with less zeal, or shrink from the bloody boldness of the other with greater timidity, because the blockhead thinks he can eat angels in muffins and chew a spiritual nature in the crumpets which he buys from the baker's shop? I am sorry there should be such impious folly in the world, but I should be ten times a greater fool than he is, if I refused, till he had made a solemn protestation that the crumpet was spiritless and the muffin nothing but a human muffin, to lead him out against the enemies of the state. Your whole argument is wrong: the state has nothing whatever to do with theological errors which do not violate the common rules of morality, and militate against the fair power of the ruler: it leaves all these errors to you, and to such as you. You have every tenth porker in your parish for refuting them; and take care that you are vigilant and logical in the task.

I love the Church as well as you do; but you totally mistake the nature of an establishment, when you contend that it ought to be connected with the military and civil career of every individual in the state. It is quite right that there should be one clergyman to every parish interpreting the Scriptures after a particular manner, ruled by a regular hierarchy, and paid with a rich proportion of haycocks and wheatsheafs. When I have laid this foundation for a rational religion in the state—when I have placed ten thousand well-educated men in different parts of the kingdom to preach it up, and compelled everybody to pay them, whether they hear them or not— I have taken such measures as I know must always procure an immense majority in favour of the Established Church; but I can go no further. I cannot set up a civil inquisition, and say to one, you shall not be a butcher, because you are not orthodox; and prohibit another from brewing, and a third from administering the law, and a fourth from defending the country. If common justice did not prohibit me from such a conduct, common sense would. The advantage to be gained by quitting the heresy would make it shameful to abandon it; and men who had once left the Church would continue in such a state of alienation from a point of honour, and transmit that spirit to their latest posterity. This is just the effect your disqualifying laws have produced. They have fed Dr. Rees, and Dr. Kippis; crowded the congregations of the Old Jewry to suffocation: and enabled every sublapsarian, and superlapsarian, and semi- pelagian clergyman, to build himself a neat brick chapel, and live with some distant resemblance to the state of a gentleman.

You say the King's coronation oath will not allow him to consent to any relaxation of the Catholic laws.—Why not relax the Catholic laws as well as the laws against Protestant dissenters? If one is contrary to his oath, the other must be so too; for the spirit of the oath is, to defend the Church establishment, which the Quaker and the Presbyterian differ from as much or more than the Catholic; and yet his Majesty has repealed the Corporation and Test Act in Ireland, and done more for the Catholics of both kingdoms than had been done for them since the Reformation. In 1778 the ministers said nothing about the royal conscience; in 1793 no conscience; in 1804 no conscience; the common feeling of humanity and justice then seem to have had their fullest influence upon the advisers of the Crown; but in 1807—a year, I suppose, eminently fruitful in moral and religious scruples (as some years are fruitful in apples, some in hops),—it is contended by the well-paid John Bowles, and by Mr. Perceval (who tried to be well paid), that this is now perjury which we had hitherto called policy and benevolence. Religious liberty has never made such a stride as under the reign of his present Majesty; nor is there any instance in the annals of our history, where so many infamous and damnable laws have been repealed as those against the Catholics which have been put an end to by him; and then, at the close of this useful policy, his advisers discover that the very measures of concession and indulgence, or (to use my own language) the measures of justice, which he has been pursuing through the whole of his reign, are contrary to the oath he takes at its commencement! That oath binds his Majesty not to consent to any measure contrary to the interest of the Established Church; but who is to judge of the tendency of each particular measure? Not the King alone: it can never be the intention of this law that the King,

13

who listens to the advice of his Parliament upon a read bill, should reject it upon the most important of all measures. Whatever be his own private judgment of the tendency of any ecclesiastical bill, he complies most strictly with his oath, if he is guided in that particular point by the advice of his Parliament, who may be presumed to understand its tendency better than the King, or any other individual. You say, if Parliament had been unanimous in their opinion of the absolute necessity for Lord Howick's bill, and the King had thought it pernicious, he would have been perjured if he had not rejected it. I say, on the contrary, his Majesty would have acted in the most conscientious manner, and have complied most scrupulously with his oath, if he had sacrificed his own opinion to the opinion of the great council of the nation; because the probability was that such opinion was better than his own; and upon the same principle, in common life, you give up your opinion to your physician, your lawyer, and your builder.

You admit this bill did not compel the King to elect Catholic officers, but only gave him the option of doing so if he pleased; but you add, that the King was right in not trusting such dangerous power to himself or his successors. Now you are either to suppose that the King for the time being has a zeal for the Catholic establishment, or that he has not. If he has not, where is the danger of giving such an option? If you suppose that he may be influenced by such an admiration of the Catholic religion, why did his present Majesty, in the year 1804, consent to that bill which empowered the Crown to station ten thousand Catholic soldiers in any part of the kingdom, and place them absolutely at the disposal of the Crown? If the King of England for the time being is a good Protestant, there can be no danger in making the Catholic ELIGIBLE to anything: if he is not, no power can possibly be so dangerous as that conveyed by the bill last quoted; to which, in point of peril, Lord Howick's bill is a mere joke. But the real fact is, one bill opened a door to his Majesty's advisers for trick, jobbing, and intrigue; the other did not.

Besides, what folly to talk to me of an oath, which, under all possible circumstances, is to prevent the relaxation of the Catholic laws! for such a solemn appeal to God sets all conditions and contingencies at defiance. Suppose Bonaparte was to retrieve the only very great blunder he has made, and were to succeed, after repeated trials, in making an impression upon Ireland, do you think we should hear any thing of the impediment of a coronation oath? or would the spirit of this country tolerate for an hour such ministers, and such unheard-of nonsense, if the most distant prospect existed of conciliating the Catholics by every species even of the most abject concession? And yet, if your argument is good for anything, the coronation oath ought to reject, at such a moment, every tendency to conciliation, and to bind Ireland for ever to the crown of France.

I found in your letter the usual remarks about fire, fagot, and bloody Mary. Are you aware, my dear Priest, that there were as many persons put to death for religious opinions under the mild Elizabeth as under the bloody Mary? The reign of the former was, to be sure, ten times as long; but I only mention the fact, merely to show you that something depends upon the age in which men live, as well as on their religious opinions. Three hundred years ago men burnt and hanged each other for these opinions. Time has softened Catholic as well as Protestant: they both required it; though each perceives only his own improvement, and is blind to that of the other. We are all the creatures of circumstances. I know not a kinder and better man than yourself; but you, if you had lived in those times, would certainly have roasted your Catholic: and I promise you, if the first exciter of this religious mob had been as powerful then as he is now, you would soon have been elevated to the mitre. I do not go the length of saying that the world has suffered as much from Protestant as from Catholic persecution; far from it: but you should remember the Catholics had all the power, when the idea first started up in the world that there could be two modes of faith; and that it was much more natural they should attempt to crush this diversity of opinion by great and cruel efforts, than that the Protestants should rage against those who differed from them, when the very basis of their system was complete freedom in all spiritual matters.

I cannot extend my letter any further at present, but you shall soon hear from me again. You tell me I am a party man. I hope I shall always be so, when I see my country in the hands of a pert London joker and a second-rate lawyer. Of the first, no other good is known than that he makes pretty Latin verses; the second seems to me to have the head of a country parson and the tongue of an Old Bailey lawyer.

If I could see good measures pursued, I care not a farthing who is in power; but I have a passionate love for common justice, and for common sense, and I abhor and despise every man who builds up his political fortune upon their ruin.

God bless you, reverend Abraham, and defend you from the Pope, and all of us from that administration who seek power by opposing a measure which Burke, Pitt, and Fox all considered as absolutely necessary to the existence of the country.

LETTER II.

Dear Abraham,—The Catholic not respect an oath! why not? What upon earth has kept him out of Parliament, or excluded him from all the offices whence he is excluded, but his respect for oaths? There is no law which prohibits a Catholic to sit in Parliament. There could be no such law; because it is impossible to find out what passes in the interior of any man's mind. Suppose it were in contemplation to exclude all men from certain offices who contended for the legality of taking tithes: the only mode of discovering that fervid love of decimation which I know you to possess would be to tender you an oath "against that damnable doctrine, that it is lawful for a spiritual man to take, abstract, appropriate, subduct, or lead away the tenth calf, sheep, lamb, ox, pigeon, duck," &c., &c., &c., and every other animal that ever existed, which of course the lawyers would take care to enumerate. Now this oath I am sure you would rather die than take; and so the Catholic is excluded from Parliament because he will not swear that he disbelieves the leading doctrines of his religion! The Catholic asks you to abolish some oaths which oppress him; your answer is that he does not respect oaths. Then why subject him to the test of oaths? The oaths keep him out of Parliament; why, then, he respects them. Turn which way you will, either your laws are nugatory, or the Catholic is bound by religious obligations as you are; but no eel in the well-sanded fist of a cook-maid, upon the eve of being skinned, ever twisted and writhed as an orthodox parson does when he is compelled by the gripe of reason to admit anything in favour of a dissenter.

I will not dispute with you whether the Pope be or be not the Scarlet Lady of Babylon. I hope it is not so; because I am afraid it will induce His Majesty's Chancellor of the

Exchequer to introduce several severe bills against popery, if that is the case; and though he will have the decency to appoint a previous committee of inquiry as to the fact, the committee will be garbled, and the report inflammatory. Leaving this to be settled as he pleases to settle it, I wish to inform you, that, previously to the bill last passed in favour of the Catholics, at the suggestion of Mr. Pitt, and for his satisfaction, the opinions of six of the most celebrated of the foreign Catholic universities were taken as to the right of the Pope to interfere in the temporal concerns of any country. The answer cannot possibly leave the shadow of a doubt, even in the mind of Baron Maseres; and Dr. Rennel would be compelled to admit it, if three Bishops lay dead at the very moment the question were put to him. To this answer might be added also the solemn declaration and signature of all the Catholics in Great Britain.

I should perfectly agree with you, if the Catholics admitted such a dangerous dispensing power in the hands of the Pope; but they all deny it, and laugh at it, and are ready to abjure it in the most decided manner you can devise. They obey the Pope as the spiritual head of their Church; but are you really so foolish as to be imposed upon by mere names? What matters it the seven-thousandth part of a farthing who is the spiritual head of any Church? Is not Mr. Wilberforce at the head of the Church of Clapham? Is not Dr. Letsom at the head of the Quaker Church? Is not the General

Assembly at the head of the Church of Scotland? How is the government disturbed by these many-headed Churches? or in what way is the power of the Crown augmented by this almost nominal dignity?

The King appoints a fast-day once a year, and he makes the bishops: and if the government would take half the pains to keep the Catholics out of the arms of France that it does to widen Temple Bar, or improve Snow Hill, the King would get into his hands the appointments of the titular Bishops of Ireland. Both Mr. C-'s sisters enjoy pensions more than sufficient to place the two greatest dignitaries of the Irish Catholic Church entirely at the disposal of the Crown.

Everybody who knows Ireland knows perfectly well, that nothing would be easier, with the expenditure of a little money, than to preserve enough of the ostensible appointment in the hands of the Pope to satisfy the scruples of the Catholics, while the real nomination remained with the Crown. But, as I have before said, the moment the very name of Ireland is mentioned, the English seem to bid adieu to common feeling, common prudence, and common sense, and to act with the barbarity of tyrants and the fatuity of idiots.

Whatever your opinion may be of the follies of the Roman Catholic religion, remember they are the follies of four millions of human beings, increasing rapidly in numbers, wealth, and intelligence, who, if firmly united with this country, would set at defiance the power of France, and if once wrested from their alliance with England, would in three years render its existence as an independent nation absolutely impossible. You speak of danger to the Establishment: I request to know when the Establishment was ever so much in danger as when Hoche was in Bantry Bay, and whether all the books of Bossuet, or the arts of the Jesuits, were half so terrible? Mr. Perceval and his parsons forget all this, in their horror lest twelve or fourteen old women may be converted to holy water and Catholic nonsense. They never see that, while they are saving these venerable ladies from perdition, Ireland may be lost, England broken down, and the Protestant Church, with all its deans, prebendaries, Percevals, and Rennels, be swept into the vortex of oblivion.

Do not, I beseech you, ever mention to me again the name of Dr. Duigenan. I have been in every corner of Ireland, and have studied its present strength and condition with no common labour. Be assured Ireland does not contain at this moment less than five millions of people. There were returned in the year 1791 to the hearth tax 701,000 houses, and there is no kind of question that there were about 50,000 houses omitted in that return. Taking, however, only the number returned for the tax, and allowing the average of six to a house (a very small average for a potato-fed people), this brings the population to

4,200,000 people in the year 1791: and it can be shown from the clearest evidence (and Mr. Newenham in his book shows it), that Ireland for the last fifty years has increased in its population at the rate of 50 or 60,000 per annum; which leaves the present population of Ireland at about five millions, after every possible deduction for EXISTING CIRCUMSTANCES, JUST AND NECESSARY WARS, MONSTROUS AND UNNATURAL REBELLIONS, and all other sources of human destruction. Of this population, two out of ten are Protestants; and the half of the Protestant population are Dissenters, and as inimical to the Church as the Catholics themselves. In this state of things thumbscrews and whipping—admirable engines of policy as they must be considered to be—will not ultimately avail. The Catholics will hang over you; they will watch for the moment, and compel you hereafter to give them ten times as much, against your will, as they would now be contented with, if it were voluntarily surrendered. Remember what happened in the American war, when Ireland compelled you to give her everything she asked, and to renounce, in the most explicit manner, your claim of Sovereignty over her. God Almighty grant the folly of these present men may not bring on such another crisis of public affairs!

What are your dangers which threaten the Establishment?—Reduce this declamation to a point, and let us understand what you mean. The most ample allowance does not calculate that there would be more than twenty members who were Roman Catholics in one house, and ten in the other, if the Catholic emancipation were carried into effect. Do you mean that these thirty members would bring in a bill to take away the tithes from the Protestant, and to pay them to the Catholic clergy? Do you mean that a Catholic general would march his army into the House of Commons, and purge it of Mr. Perceval and Dr. Duigenan? or, that the theological writers would become all of a sudden more acute or more learned, if the present civil incapacities were removed? Do you fear for your tithes, or your doctrines, or your person, or the English Constitution? Every fear, taken separately, is so glaringly absurd, that no man has the folly or the boldness to state it. Every one conceals his ignorance, or his baseness, in a stupid general panic, which, when called on, he is utterly incapable of explaining. Whatever you think of the Catholics, there they are—you cannot get rid of them; your alternative is to give them a lawful place for stating their grievances, or an unlawful one: if you do not admit them to the House of Commons, they will hold their parliament in Potatoe Place, Dublin, and be ten times as violent and inflammatory as they would be in Westminster. Nothing would give me such an idea of security as to see twenty or thirty Catholic gentlemen in Parliament, looked upon by all the Catholics as the fair and proper organ of their party. I should have thought it the height of good fortune that such a wish existed on their part, and the very essence of madness and ignorance to reject it. Can you murder the Catholics? Can you neglect them? They are too numerous for both these expedients. What remains to be done is obvious to every human being—but to that man who, instead of being a Methodist preacher, is, for the curse of us and our children, and for the ruin of Troy and the misery of good old Priam and his sons, become a legislator and a politician.

A distinction, I perceive, is taken by one of the most feeble noblemen in Great Britain, between persecution and the deprivation of political power; whereas, there is no more distinction between these two things than there is between him who makes the distinction and a booby. If I strip off the relic-covered jacket of a Catholic, and give him twenty stripes . . . I persecute; if I say, Everybody in the town where you live shall be a candidate for lucrative and honourable offices, but you, who are a Catholic . . . I do not persecute! What barbarous nonsense is this! as if degradation was not as great an evil as bodily pain or as severe poverty: as if I could not be as great a tyrant by saying, You shall not enjoy—as by saying, You shall suffer. The English, I believe, are as truly religious as any nation in Europe; I know no greater blessing; but it carries with it this evil in its train, that any villain who will bawl out, "The Church is in danger!" may get a place and a good pension; and that any administration who will do the same thing may bring a set of men into power who, at a moment of stationary and passive piety, would be hooted by the very boys in the streets. But it is not all religion; it is, in great part, the narrow and exclusive spirit which delights to keep the common blessings of sun and air and freedom from other human beings. "Your religion has always been degraded; you are in the dust, and I will take care you never rise again. I should enjoy less the possession of an earthly good by every additional person to whom it was extended." You may not be aware of it yourself, most reverend Abraham, but you deny their freedom to the Catholics upon the same principle that Sarah your wife refuses to give the receipt for a ham or a gooseberry dumpling: she values her receipts, not because they secure to her a certain flavour, but because they remind her that her neighbours want it:- a feeling laughable in a priestess, shameful in a priest; venial when it withholds the blessings of a ham, tyrannical and execrable when it narrows the boon of religious freedom.

You spend a great deal of ink about the character of the present prime minister. Grant you all that you write—I say, I fear he will ruin Ireland, and pursue a line of policy destructive to the true interest of his country: and then you tell me, he is faithful to Mrs. Perceval, and kind to the Master Percevals! These are, undoubtedly, the first qualifications to be looked to in a time of the most serious public danger; but somehow or another (if public and private virtues must always be incompatible), I should prefer that he destroyed the domestic happiness of Wood or Cockell, owed for the veal of the preceding year, whipped his boys, and saved his country.

The late administration did not do right; they did not build their measures upon the solid basis of facts. They should have caused several Catholics to have been dissected after death by surgeons of either religion; and the report to have been published with accompanying plates. If the viscera, and other organs of life, had been found to be the same as in Protestant bodies; if the provisions of nerves, arteries, cerebrum, and cerebellum, had been the same as we are provided with, or as the Dissenters are now known to possess; then, indeed, they might have met Mr. Perceval upon a proud eminence, and convinced the country at large of the strong probability that the Catholics are really human creatures, endowed with the feelings of men, and entitled to all their rights. But instead of this wise and prudent measure, Lord Howick, with his usual precipitation, brings forward a bill in their favour, without offering the slightest proof to the country that they were anything more than horses and oxen. The person who shows the lama at the corner of Piccadilly has the precaution to write up—ALLOWED BY SIR JOSEPH BANKS TO BE A REAL QUADRUPED, so his Lordship might have said—ALLOWED BY THE BENCH OF BISHOPS TO BE REAL HUMAN CREATURES. . . . I could write you twenty letters upon this subject; but I am tired, and so I suppose are you. Our friendship is now of forty years' standing; you know me to be a truly religious man; but I shudder to see religion treated like a cockade, or a pint of beer, and made the instrument of a party. I love the king, but I love the people as well as the king; and if I am sorry to see his old age molested, I am much more sorry to see four millions of Catholics baffled in their just expectations. If I love Lord Grenville, and Lord Howick, it is because they love their country; if I abhor . . . it is because I know there is but one man among them who is not laughing at the enormous folly and credulity of the country, and that he is an ignorant and mischievous bigot. As for the light and frivolous jester, of whom it is your misfortune to think so highly, learn, my dear Abraham, that this political Killigrew, just before the breaking-up of the last administration, was in actual treaty with them for a place; and if they had survived twenty-four hours longer, he would have been now declaiming against the cry of No Popery! instead of inflaming it. With this practical comment on the baseness of human nature, I bid you adieu!

LETTER III.

All that I have so often told you, Mr. Abraham Plymley, is now come to pass. The Scythians, in whom you and the neighbouring country gentleman placed such confidence, are smitten hip and thigh; their Beningsen put to open shame; their magazines of train oil intercepted, and we are waking from our disgraceful drunkenness to all the horrors of Mr. Perceval and Mr Canning . . . We shall now see if a nation is to be saved by school-boy jokes and doggrel rhymes, by affronting petulance, and by the tones and gesticulations of Mr. Pitt. But these are not all the auxiliaries on which we have to depend; to these his colleague will add the strictest attention to the smaller parts of ecclesiastical government, to hassocks, to psalters, and to surplices; in the last agonies of England, he will bring in a bill to regulate Easter-offerings: and he will adjust the stipends of curates, when the flag of France is unfurled on the hills of Kent. Whatever can be done by very mistaken notions of the piety of a Christian, and by a very wretched imitation of the eloquence of Mr. Pitt, will be done by these two gentlemen. After all, if they both really were what they both either wish to be, or wish to be thought; if the one were an enlightened Christian who drew from the Gospel the toleration, the charity, and the sweetness which it contains; and if the other really possessed any portion of the great understanding of his Nisus who guarded him from the weapons of the Whigs, I should still doubt if they could save us. But I am sure we are not to be saved by religious hatred, and by religious trifling; by any psalmody, however sweet; or by any persecution, however sharp; I am certain the sounds of Mr. Pitt's voice, and the measure of his tones, and the movement of his arms, will do nothing for us; when these tones and movements, and voice brings us always declamation without sense or knowledge, and ridicule without good humour or conciliation. Oh, Mr. Plymley, this never will do. Mrs. Abraham Plymley, my sister, will be led away captive by an amorous Gaul; and Joel Plymley your firstborn, will be a French drummer.

Out of sight, out of mind, seems to be a proverb which applies to enemies as well as friends. Because the French army was no longer seen from the cliffs of Dover; because the sound of cannon was no longer heard by the debauched London bathers on the Sussex coast; because the Morning Post no longer fixed the invasion sometimes for Monday, sometimes for Tuesday, sometimes (positively for the last time of invading) on Saturday; because all these causes of terror were suspended, you conceived the power of Bonaparte to be at an end, and were setting off for Paris with Lord Hawkesbury the conqueror. This is precisely the method in which the English have acted during the whole of the revolutionary war. If Austria or Prussia armed, doctors of divinity immediately printed those passages out of Habakkuk, in which the destruction of the Usurper by General Mack, and the Duke of Brunswick, are so clearly predicted. If Bonaparte halted, there was a mutiny or a dysentery. If any one of his generals were eaten up by the light troops of Russia, and picked (as their manner is) to the bone, the sanguine spirit of this country displayed itself in all its glory. What scenes of infamy did the Society for the Suppression of Vice lay open to our astonished eyes! tradesmen's daughters dancing, pots of beer carried out between the first and second lesson, and dark and distant rumours of indecent prints. Clouds of Mr. Canning's cousins arrived by the waggon; all the contractors left their cards with Mr. Rose; and every plunderer of the public crawled out of his hole, like slugs, and grubs, and worms after a shower of rain.

If my voice could have been heard at the late changes, I should have said, "Gently, patience, stop a little; the time is not yet come; the mud of Poland will harden, and the bowels of the French grenadiers will recover their tone. When honesty, good sense, and liberality have extricated you out of your present embarrassment, then dismiss them as a matter of course; but you cannot spare them just now; don't be in too great a hurry, or there will be no monarch to flatter, and no country to pillage; only submit for a little time to be respected abroad, overlook the painful absence of the tax-gatherer for a few years, bear up nobly under the increase of freedom and of liberal policy for a little time, and I promise you, at the expiration of that period, you shall be plundered, insulted, disgraced, and restrained to your heart's content. Do not imagine I have any intention of putting servility and canting hypocrisy permanently out of place, or of filling up with courage and sense those offices which naturally devolve upon decorous imbecility and flexible cunning: give us only a little time to keep off the hussars of France, and then the jobbers and jesters shall return to their birthright, and public virtue be called by its own name of fanaticism." Such is the advice I would have offered to my infatuated countrymen: but it rained very hard in November, Brother Abraham, and the bowels of our enemies were loosened, and we put our trust in white fluxes and wet mud; and there is nothing now to oppose to the conqueror of the world but a small table wit, and the sallow Surveyor of the Meltings.

You ask me, if I think it possible for this country to survive the recent misfortunes of Europe?—I answer you, without the slightest degree of hesitation: that if Bonaparte lives, and a great deal is not immediately done for the conciliation of the Catholics, it does seem to me absolutely impossible but that we must perish; and take this with you, that we shall perish without exciting the slightest feeling of present or future compassion, but fall amidst the hootings and revilings of Europe, as a nation of blockheads, Methodists, and old women. If there were any great scenery, any heroic feelings, any blaze of ancient virtue, any exalted death, any termination of England that would be ever remembered, ever honoured in that western world, where liberty is now retiring, conquest would be more tolerable, and ruin more sweet; but it is doubly miserable to become slaves abroad, because we would be tyrants at home; to persecute, when we are contending against persecution; and to perish, because we have raised up worse enemies within, from our own bigotry, than we are exposed to without, from the unprincipled ambition of France. It is indeed a most silly and affecting spectacle to rage at such a moment against our own kindred and our own blood; to tell them they cannot be honourable in war, because they are conscientious in religion; to stipulate (at the very moment when we should buy their hearts and swords at any price) that they must hold up the right hand in prayer, and not the left; and adore one common God, by turning to the east rather than to the west.

What is it the Catholics ask of you? Do not exclude us from the honours and emoluments of the state because we worship God in one way, and you worship Him in another. In a period of the deepest peace, and the fattest prosperity, this would be a fair request; it should be granted, if Lord Hawkesbury had reached Paris, if Mr. Canning's interpreter had threatened the Senate in an opening speech, or Mr. Perceval explained to them the improvements he meant to introduce into the Catholic religion; but to deny the Irish this justice now, in the present state of Europe, and in the summer months, just as the season for destroying kingdoms is coming on, is (beloved Abraham), whatever you may think of it, little short of positive insanity.

Here is a frigate attacked by a corsair of immense strength and size, rigging cut, masts in danger of coming by the board, four foot water in the hold, men dropping off very fast; in this dreadful situation how do you think the Captain acts (whose name shall be Perceval)? He calls all hands upon deck; talks to them of King, country, glory, sweethearts, gin, French prison, wooden shoes, Old England, and hearts of oak; they give three cheers, rush to their guns, and, after a tremendous conflict, succeed in beating off the enemy. Not a syllable of all this; this is not the manner in which the honourable Commander goes to work: the first thing he does is to secure twenty or thirty of his prime sailors who happen to be Catholics, to clap them in irons, and set over them a guard of as many Protestants; having taken this admirable method of defending himself against his infidel opponents, he goes upon deck, reminds the sailors in a very bitter harangue, that they are of different religions; exhorts the Episcopal gunner not to trust to the Presbyterian quartermaster; issues positive orders that the Catholics should be fired at upon the first appearance of discontent; rushes through blood and brains, examining his men in the Catechism and thirty-nine Articles, and positively forbids every one to sponge or ram who has not taken the Sacrament according to the Church of England. Was it right to take out a captain made of excellent British stuff, and to put in such a man as this? Is not he more like a parson, or a talking lawyer, than a thorough-bred seaman? And built as she is of heart of oak, and admirably manned, is it possible, with such a captain, to save this ship from going to the bottom?

You have an argument, I perceive, in common with many others, against the Catholics, that their demands complied with would only lead to further exactions, and that it is better to resist them now, before anything is conceded, than hereafter, when it is found that all concessions are in vain. I wish the Chancellor of the Exchequer, who uses this reasoning to exclude others from their just rights, had tried its efficacy, not by his understanding, but by (what are full of much better things) his pockets. Suppose the person to whom he applied for the meltings had withstood every plea of wife and fourteen children, no business, and good character, and refused him this paltry little office because he might hereafter attempt to get hold of the revenues of the Duchy of Lancaster for life? would not Mr. Perceval have contended eagerly against the injustice of refusing moderate requests, because immoderate ones may hereafter be made? Would he not have said, and said truly, Leave such exorbitant attempts as these to the general indignation of the Commons, who will take care to defeat them when they do occur; but do not refuse me the Irons and the Meltings now, because I may totally lose sight of all moderation hereafter? Leave hereafter to the spirit and the wisdom of hereafter; and do not be niggardly now from the apprehension that men as wise as you should be profuse in times to come.

You forget, Brother Abraham, that is a vast art, where quarrels cannot be avoided, to turn public opinion in your favour and to the prejudice of your enemy; a vast privilege to feel that you are in the right, and to make him feel that he is in the wrong: a privilege which makes you more than a man, and your antagonist less; and often secures victory by convincing him who contends that he must submit to injustice if he submits to defeat. Open every rank in the army and the navy to the Catholic; let him purchase at the same price as the Protestant (if either Catholic or Protestant can purchase such refined pleasures) the privilege of hearing Lord Castlereagh speak for three hours; keep his clergy from starving, soften some of the most odious powers of the tithing-man, and you will for ever lay this formidable question to rest. But if I am wrong, and you must quarrel at last, quarrel upon just rather than unjust grounds; divide the Catholic and unite the Protestant; be just, and your own exertions will be more formidable and their exertions less formidable; be just, and you will take away from their party all the best and wisest understandings of both persuasions, and knit them firmly to your own cause. "Thrice is he armed who has his quarrel just;" and ten times as much may he be taxed. In the beginning of any war, however destitute of common sense, every mob will roar, and every Lord of the

Bedchamber address; but if you are engaged in a war that is to last for years, and to require important sacrifices, take care to make the justice of your case so clear and so obvious that it cannot be mistaken by the most illiterate country gentleman who rides the earth. Nothing, in fact, can be so grossly absurd as the argument which says I will deny justice to you now, because I suspect future injustice from you. At this rate, you may lock a man up in your stable, and refuse to let him out, because you suspect that he has an intention, at some future period, of robbing your hen-roost. You may horsewhip him at Lady Day, because you believe he will affront you at Midsummer. You may commit a greater evil, to guard against a less which is merely contingent, and may never happen. You may do what you have done a century ago in Ireland, make the Catholics worse than Helots, because you suspected that they might hereafter aspire to be more than fellow citizens; rendering their sufferings certain from your jealousy, while yours were only doubtful from their ambition; an ambition sure to be excited by the very measures which were taken to prevent it.

The physical strength of the Catholics will not be greater because you give them a share of political power. You may by these means turn rebels into friends; but I do not see how you make rebels more formidable. If they taste of the honey of lawful power, they will love the hive from whence they procure it; if they will struggle with us like men in the

36

same state for civil influence, we are safe. All that I dread is the physical strength of four millions of men combined with an invading French army. If you are to quarrel at last with this enormous population, still put it off as long as you can; you must gain, and cannot lose, by the delay. The state of Europe cannot be worse; the conviction which the Catholics entertain of your tyranny and injustice cannot be more alarming, nor the opinions of your own people more divided. Time, which produces such effect upon brass and marble, may inspire one Minister with modesty and another with compassion; every circumstance may be better; some certainly will be so, none can be worse; and after all the evil may never happen.

You have got hold, I perceive, of all the vulgar English stories respecting the hereditary transmission of forfeited property, and seriously believe that every Catholic beggar wears the terriers of his father's land next his skin, and is only waiting for better times to cut the throat of the Protestant possessor, and get drunk in the hall of his ancestors. There is one irresistible answer to this mistake, and that is, that the forfeited lands are purchased indiscriminately by Catholic and Protestant, and that the Catholic purchaser never objects to such a title. Now the land so purchased by a Catholic is either his own family estate, or it is not. If it is, you suppose him so desirous of coming into possession that he resorts to the double method of rebellion and purchase; if it is not his own family estate of which he becomes the purchaser, you suppose him first to purchase, then to rebel, in order to defeat the purchase. These things may happen in Ireland, but it is totally impossible they can happen anywhere else. In fact, what land can any man of any sect purchase in Ireland, but forfeited property? In all other oppressed countries which I have ever heard of, the rapacity of the conqueror was bounded by the territorial limits in which the objects of his avarice were contained; but Ireland has been actually confiscated twice over, as a cat is twice killed by a wicked parish boy.

I admit there is a vast luxury in selecting a particular set of Christians, and in worrying them as a boy worries a puppy dog; it is an amusement in which all the young English are brought up from their earliest days. I like the idea of saying to men who use a different hassock from me, that till they change their hassock they shall never be Colonels, Aldermen, or Parliament-men. While I am gratifying my personal insolence respecting religious forms, I fondle myself into an idea that I am religious, and that I am doing my duty in the most exemplary, as I certainly am in the most easy, way. But then, my good Abraham, this sport, admirable as it is, is become, with respect to the Catholics, a little dangerous; and if we are not extremely careful in taking the amusement, we shall tumble into the holy water and be drowned. As it seems necessary to your idea of an established church to have somebody to worry and torment, suppose we were to select for this purpose William Wilberforce, Esq., and the patent Christians of Clapham. We shall by this expedient enjoy the same opportunity for cruelty and injustice, without being exposed to the same risks: we will compel them to abjure vital clergymen by a public test, to deny that the said William Wilberforce has any power of working miracles, touching for barrenness or any other infirmity, or that he is endowed with any preternatural gift whatever. We will swear them to the doctrine of good works, compel them to preach common sense, and to hear it; to frequent Bishops, Deans, and other High Churchmen; and to appear, once in the quarter at the least, at some melodrame, opera, pantomime, or other light scenical representation; in short, we will gratify the love of insolence and power; we will enjoy the old orthodox sport of witnessing the impotent anger of men compelled to submit to civil degradation, or to sacrifice their notions of truth to ours. And all this we may do without the slightest risk, because their numbers are, as yet, not very considerable. Cruelty and injustice must, of course, exist; but why connect them with danger? Why torture a bulldog when you can get a frog or a rabbit? I am sure my proposal will meet with the most universal approbation. Do not be apprehensive of any opposition from ministers. If it is a case of hatred, we are sure that one man will defend it by the Gospel: if it abridges human freedom, we know that another will find precedents for it in the Revolution.

In the name of Heaven, what are we to gain by suffering Ireland to be rode by that faction which now predominates over it? Why are we to endanger our own Church and State, not for 500,000 Episcopalians, but for ten or twelve great Orange families, who have been sucking the blood of that country for these hundred years last past? and the folly of the Orangemen in playing this game themselves, is almost as absurd as ours in playing it for them. They ought to have the sense to see that their business now is to keep quietly the lands and beeves of which the fathers of the Catholics were robbed in days of yore; they must give to their descendants the sop of political power: by contending with them for names, they will lose realities, and be compelled to beg their potatoes in a foreign land, abhorred equally by the English, who have witnessed their oppression, and by the Catholic Irish, who have smarted under them.

LETTER IV.

Then comes Mr. Isaac Hawkins Brown (the gentleman who danced so badly at the Court of Naples), and asks if it is not an anomaly to educate men in another religion than your own. It certainly is our duty to get rid of error, and, above all, of religious error; but this is not to be done per saltum, or the measure will miscarry, like the Queen. It may be very easy to dance away the royal embryo of a great kingdom; but Mr. Hawkins Brown must look before he leaps, when his object is to crush an opposite sect in religion; false steps aid the one effect as much as they are fatal to the other: it will require not only the lapse of Mr. Hawkins Brown, but the lapse of centuries, before the absurdities of the Catholic religion are laughed at as much as they deserve to be; but surely, in the meantime, the Catholic religion is better than none; four millions of Catholics are better than four millions of wild beasts; two hundred priests educated by our own government are better than the same number educated by the man who means to destroy us.

The whole sum now appropriated by Government to the religious education of four millions of Christians is 13,000 pounds; a sum about one hundred times as large being appropriated in the same country to about one-eighth part of this number of Protestants. When it was proposed to raise this grant from 8,000 pounds to 13,000 pounds, its present amount, this sum was objected to by that most indulgent of Christians, Mr. Spencer Perceval, as enormous; he himself having secured for his own eating and drinking, and the eating and drinking of the Master and Miss Percevals, the reversionary sum of 21,000 pounds a year of the public money, and having just failed in a desperate and rapacious attempt to secure to himself for life the revenues of the Duchy of Lancaster: and the best of it is, that this minister, after abusing his predecessors for their impious bounty to the Catholics, has found himself compelled, from the apprehension of immediate danger, to grant the sum in question, thus dissolving his pearl in vinegar, and destroying all the value of the gift by the virulence and reluctance with which it was granted.

I hear from some persons in Parliament, and from others in the sixpenny societies for debate, a great deal about unalterable laws passed at the Revolution. When I hear any man talk of an unalterable law, the only effect it produces upon me is to convince me that he is an unalterable fool. A law passed when there was Germany, Spain, Russia, Sweden, Holland, Portugal, and Turkey; when there was a disputed succession; when four or five hundred acres were won and lost after ten years' hard fighting; when armies were commanded by the sons of kings, and campaigns passed in an interchange of civil letters and ripe fruit; and for these laws, when the whole state of the world is completely changed, we are now, according to my Lord Hawkesbury, to hold ourselves ready to perish. It is no mean misfortune, in times like these, to be forced to say anything about such men as Lord Hawkesbury, and to be reminded that we are governed by them, but as I am driven to it, I must take the liberty of observing that the wisdom and liberality of my Lord Hawkesbury are of that complexion which always shrinks from the present exercise of these virtues by praising the splendid examples of them in ages past. If he had lived at such periods, he would have opposed the Revolution by praising the Reformation, and the Reformation by speaking handsomely of the Crusades. He gratifies his natural antipathy to great and courageous measures by playing off the wisdom and courage which have ceased to influence human affairs against that wisdom and courage which living men would employ for present happiness. Besides, it happens unfortunately for the Warden of the Cinque Ports, that to the principal incapacities under which the Irish suffer, they were subjected after that great and glorious revolution, to which we are indebted for so many blessings, and his Lordship for the termination of so many periods. The Catholics were not excluded from the Irish House of Commons, or military commands, before the 3rd and 4th of William and Mary, and the 1st and 2nd of Queen Anne.

If the great mass of the people, environed as they are on every side with Jenkinsons, Percevals, Melvilles, and other perils, were to pray for divine illumination and aid, what more could Providence in its mercy do than send them the example of Scotland? For what a length of years was it attempted to compel the Scotch to change their religion: horse, foot, artillery, and armed Prebendaries, were sent out after the Presbyterian parsons and their congregations. The

Percevals of those days called for blood: this call is never made in vain, and blood was shed; but, to the astonishment and horror of the Percevals of those days, they could not introduce the book of Common Prayer, nor prevent that metaphysical people from going to heaven their true way, instead of our true way. With a little oatmeal for food, and a little sulphur for friction, allaying cutaneous irritation with the one hand, and holding his Calvinistical creed in the other, Sawney ran away to his flinty hills, sung his psalm out of tune his own way, and listened to his sermon of two hours long, amid the rough and imposing melancholy of the tallest thistles. But Sawney brought up his unbreeched offspring in a cordial hatred of his oppressors; and Scotland was as much a part of the weakness of England then as Ireland is at this moment. The true and the only remedy was applied; the Scotch were suffered to worship God after their own tiresome manner, without pain, penalty, or privation. No lightning descended from heaven: the country was not ruined; the world is not yet come to an end; the dignitaries who foretold all these consequences are utterly forgotten, and Scotland has ever since been an increasing source of strength to Great Britain. In the six hundredth year of our empire over Ireland we are making laws to transport a man if he is found out of his house after eight o'clock at night. That this is necessary I know too well; but tell me why it is necessary. It is not necessary in Greece, where the Turks are masters.

Are you aware that there is at this moment a universal clamour throughout the whole of Ireland against the Union? It is now one month since I returned from that country; I have never seen so extraordinary, so alarming, and so rapid a change in the sentiments of any people. Those who disliked the Union before are quite furious against it now; those who doubted doubt no more; those who were friendly to it have exchanged that friendship for the most rooted aversion; in the midst of all this (which is by far the most alarming symptom), there is the strongest disposition on the part of the northern Dissenters to unite with the Catholics, irritated by the faithless injustice with which they have been treated. If this combination does take place (mark what I say to you), you will have meetings all over Ireland for the cry of No Union; that cry will spread like wild-fire, and blaze over every opposition; and if this be the case, there is no use in mincing the matter; Ireland is gone, and the death-blow of England is struck; and this event may happen INSTANTLY—before Mr. Canning and Mr. Hookham Frere have turned Lord Howick's last speech into doggerel rhymne; before "the near and dear relations" have received another quarter of their pension, or Mr. Perceval conducted the Curates' Salary Bill safely to a third reading. If the mind of the English people, cursed as they now are with that madness of religious dissension which has been breathed into them for the purposes of private ambition, can be alarmed by any remembrances, and warned by any events, they should never forget how nearly Ireland was lost to this country during the American war; that it was saved merely by the jealousy of the Protestant Irish towards the Catholics, then a much more insignificant and powerless body than they now are. The Catholic and the Dissenter have since combined together against you. Last war, the winds, those ancient and unsubsidised allies of England; the winds, upon which English ministers depend as much for saving kingdoms as washerwomen do for drying clothes; the winds stood your friends: the French could only get into Ireland in small numbers, and the rebels were defeated. Since then, all the remaining kingdoms of Europe have been destroyed; and the Irish see that their national independence is gone, without having received any single one of those advantages which they were taught to expect from the sacrifice. All good things were to flow from the Union; they have none of them gained anything. Every man's pride is wounded by it; no man's interest is promoted. In the seventh year of that union four million Catholics, lured by all kinds of promises to yield up the separate dignity and sovereignty of their country, are forced to squabble with such a man as Mr. Spencer Perceval for five thousand pounds with which to educate their children in their own mode of worship, he, the same Mr. Spencer, having secured to his own Protestant self a reversionary portion of the public money amounting to four times that sum. A senior Proctor of the University of Oxford, the head of a house, or the examining chaplain to a bishop, may believe these things can last; but every man of the world, whose understanding has been exercised in the business of life, must see (and see with a breaking heart) that they will soon come to a fearful termination.

Our conduct to Ireland during the whole of this war has been that of a man who subscribes to hospitals, weeps at charity sermons, carries out broth and blankets to beggars, and then comes home and beats his wife and children. We had compassion for the victims of all other oppression and injustice except our own. If Switzerland was threatened, away went a Treasury Clerk with a hundred thousand pounds for Switzerland; large bags of money were kept constantly under sailing orders; upon the slightest demonstration towards Naples, down went Sir William Hamilton upon his knees, and begged for the love of St. Januarius they would help us off with a little money; all the arts of Machiavel were resorted to to persuade Europe to borrow; troops were sent off in all directions to save the Catholic and Protestant world; the Pope himself was guarded by a regiment of English dragoons; if the Grand Lama had been at hand, he would have had another; every Catholic clergyman who had the good fortune to be neither English nor Irish was immediately provided with lodging, soap, crucifix, missal, chapel-beads, relics, and holy water; if Turks had landed, Turks would have received an order from the Treasury for coffee, opium, korans, and seraglios. In the midst of all this fury of saving and defending this crusade for conscience and Christianity, there was a universal agreement among all descriptions of people to continue every species of internal persecution, to deny at home every just right that had been denied before, to pummel poor Dr. Abraham Rees and his Dissenters, and to treat the unhappy Catholics of Ireland as if their tongues were mute, their heels cloven, their nature brutal, and designedly subjected by Providence to their Orange masters.

How would my admirable brother, the Rev. Abraham Plymley, like to be marched to a Catholic chapel, to be sprinkled with the sanctified contents of a pump, to hear a number of false quantities in the Latin tongue, and to see a number of persons occupied in making right angles upon the breast and forehead? And if all this would give you so much pain, what right have you to march Catholic soldiers to a place of worship, where there is no aspersion, no rectangular gestures, and where they understand every word they hear, having first, in order to get him to enlist, made a solemn promise to the contrary? Can you wonder, after this, that the Catholic priest stops the recruiting in Ireland, as he is now doing to a most alarming degree?

The late question concerning military rank did not individually affect the lowest persons of the Catholic persuasion; but do you imagine they do not sympathise with the honour and disgrace of their superiors? Do you think that satisfaction and dissatisfaction do not travel down from Lord Fingal to the most potato-less Catholic in Ireland, and that the glory or shame of the sect is not felt by many more than these conditions personally and corporeally affect? Do you suppose that the detection of Sir Henry Mildmay, and the disappointment of Mr. Perceval IN THE MATTER of the Duchy of Lancaster, did not affect every dabbler in public property? Depend upon it these things were felt through all the gradations of small plunderers, down to him who filches a pound of tobacco from the King's warehouses; while, on the contrary, the acquittal of any noble and official thief would not fail to diffuse the most heart- felt satisfaction over the larcenous and burglarious world. Observe, I do not say because the lower Catholics are affected by what concerns their superiors, that they are not affected by what concerns themselves. There is no disguising the horrid truth, THERE MUST BE SOME RELAXATION WITH RESPECT TO TITHE: this is the cruel and heart-rending price which must be paid for national preservation. I feel how little existence will be worth having, if any alteration, however slight, is made in the property of Irish rectors; I am conscious how much such changes must affect the daily and hourly comforts of every Englishman; I shall feel too happy if they leave Europe untouched, and are not ultimately fatal to the destinies of America; but I am madly bent upon keeping foreign enemies out of the British empire, and my limited understanding presents me with no other means of effecting my object.

You talk of waiting till another reign before any alteration is made; a proposal full of good sense and good nature, if the measure in question were to pull down St. James's Palace, or to alter Kew Gardens. Will Bonaparte agree to put off his intrigues, and his invasion of Ireland? If so, I will overlook the question of justice, and finding the danger suspended, agree to the delay. I sincerely hope this reign may last many years, yet the delay of a single session of Parliament may be fatal; but if another year elapse without some serious concession made to the Catholics, I believe, before God, that all future pledges and concessions will be made in vain. I do not think that peace will do you any good under such circumstances. If Bonaparte give you a respite, it will only be to get ready the gallows on which he means to hang you. The Catholic and the Dissenter can unite in peace as well as war. If they do, the gallows is ready, and your executioner, in spite of the most solemn promises, will turn you off the next hour.

With every disposition to please (where to please within fair and rational limits is a high duty), it is impossible for public men to be long silent about the Catholics; pressing evils are not got rid of, because they are not talked of. A man may command his family to say nothing more about the stone and surgical operations; but the ponderous malice still lies upon the nerve, and gets so big, that the patient breaks his own law of silence, clamours for the knife, and expires under its late operation. Believe me, you talk folly when you talk of suppressing the Catholic question. I wish to God the case admitted of such a remedy; bad as it is, it does not admit of it. If the wants of the Catholics are not heard in the manly tones of Lord Grenville, or the servile drawl of Lord Castlereagh, they will be heard ere long in the madness of mobs, and the conflicts of armed men.

I observe it is now universally the fashion to speak of the first personage in the state as the great obstacle to the measure. In the first place, I am not bound to believe such rumours because I hear them; and in the next place, I object to such language, as unconstitutional. Whoever retains his situation in the ministry while the incapacities of the Catholics remain, is the advocate for those incapacities; and to him, and to him only, am I to look for responsibility. But waive this question of the Catholics, and put a general case: —How is a minister of this country to act when the conscientious scruples of his Sovereign prevent the execution of a measure deemed by him absolutely necessary to the safety of the country? His conduct is quite clear—he should resign. But what is his successor to do?—Resign. But is the King to be left without ministers, and is he in this manner to be compelled to act against his own conscience? Before I answer this, pray tell me in my turn what better defence is there against the machinations of a wicked, or the errors of a weak Monarch, than the impossibility of finding a minister who will lend himself to vice and folly? Every English Monarch, in such a predicament, would sacrifice his opinions and views to such a clear expression of the public will; and it is one method in which the Constitution aims at bringing about such a sacrifice. You may say, if you please, the ruler of a state is forced to give up his object when the natural love of place and power will tempt no one to assist him in its attainment; this may be force; but it is force without injury, and therefore without blame. I am not to be beat out of these obvious reasonings, and ancient constitutional provisions, by the term conscience. There is no fantasy, however wild, that a man may not persuade himself that he cherishes from motives of conscience; eternal war against impious France, or rebellious America, or Catholic Spain, may in times to come be scruples of conscience. One English Monarch may, from scruples of conscience, wish to abolish every trait of religious persecution; another Monarch may deem it his absolute and indispensable duty to make a slight provision for Dissenters out of the revenues of the Church of England. So that you see, Brother Abraham, there are cases where it would be the duty of the best and most loyal subjects to oppose the conscientious scruples of their Sovereign, still taking care that their actions were constitutional and their modes respectful. Then you come upon me with personal questions, and say that no such dangers are to be apprehended now under our present gracious Sovereign, of whose good qualities we must be all so well convinced. All these sorts of discussions I beg leave to decline. What I have said upon constitutional topics, I mean of course for general, not for particular application. I agree with you in all the good you have said of the powers that be, and I avail myself of the opportunity of pointing out general dangers to the Constitution, at a moment when we are so completely exempted from their present influence. I cannot finish this letter without expressing my surprise and pleasure at your abuse of the servile addresses poured in upon the throne, nor can I conceive a greater disgust to a Monarch, with a true English heart, than to see such a question as that of Catholic Emancipation argued, not with a reference to its justice or importance, but universally considered to be of no further consequence than as it affects his own private feelings. That these sentiments should be mine is not wonderful; but how they came to be yours does, I confess, fill me with surprise. Are you moved by the arrival of the Irish Brigade at Antwerp, and the amorous violence which awaits Mrs. Plymley?

LETTER V.

Dear Abraham,—I never met a parson in my life who did not consider the Corporation and Test Acts as the great bulwarks of the Church; and yet it is now just sixty-four years since bills of indemnity to destroy their penal effects, or, in other words, to repeal them, have been passed annually as a matter of course.

Heu vatum ignar mentes.

These bulwarks, without which no clergyman thinks he could sleep with his accustomed soundness, have actually not been in existence since any man now living has taken holy orders. Every year the Indemnity Act pardons past breaches of these two laws, and prevents any fresh actions of informers from coming to a conclusion before the period for the next indemnity bill arrives; so that these penalties, by which alone the Church remains in existence, have not had one moment's operation for sixty-four years. You will say the legislature, during the whole of this period, has reserved to itself the discretion of suspending or not suspending. But had not the legislature the right of re-enacting, if it was necessary? And now when you have kept the rod over these people (with the most scandalous abuse of all principle) for sixty-four years, and not found it necessary to strike once, is not that the best of all reasons why the rod should be laid aside? You talk to me of a very valuable hedge running across your fields which you would not part with on any account. I go down, expecting to find a limit impervious to cattle, and highly useful for the preservation of property; but, to my utter astonishment, I find that the hedge was cut down half a century ago, and that every year the shoots are clipped the moment they appear above ground: it appears, upon further inquiry, that the hedge never ought to have existed at all; that it originated in the malice of antiquated quarrels, and was cut down because it subjected you to vast inconvenience, and broke up your intercourse with a country absolutely necessary to your existence. If the remains of this hedge serve only to keep up an irritation in your neighbours, and to remind them of the feuds of former times, good nature and good sense teach you that you ought to grub it up, and cast it into the oven. This is the exact state of these two laws; and yet it is made a great argument against concession to the Catholics, that it involves their repeal; which is to say, Do not make me relinquish a folly that will lead to my ruin; because, if you do, I must give up other follies ten times greater than this.

I confess, with all our bulwarks and hedges, it mortifies me to the quick to contrast with our matchless stupidity and inimitable folly the conduct of Bonaparte upon the subject of religious persecution. At the moment when we are tearing the crucifixes from the necks of the Catholics, and washing pious mud from the foreheads of the Hindoos;

at that moment this man is assembling the very Jews at Paris, and endeavouring to give them stability and importance. I shall never be reconciled to mending shoes in America; but I see it must be my lot, and I will then take a dreadful revenge upon Mr. Perceval, if I catch him preaching within ten miles of me. I cannot for the soul of me conceive whence this man has gained his notions of Christianity: he has the most evangelical charity for errors in arithmetic, and the most inveterate malice against errors in conscience. While he rages against those whom in the true spirit of the Gospel he ought to indulge, he forgets the only instance of severity which that Gospel contains, and leaves the jobbers, contractors, and money-changers at their seats, without a single stripe.

You cannot imagine, you say, that England will ever be ruined and conquered; and for no other reason that I can find, but because it seems so very odd it should be ruined and conquered. Alas! so reasoned, in their time, the Austrian, Russian, and Prussian Plymleys. But the English are brave: so were all these nations. You might get together a hundred thousand men individually brave; but without generals capable of commanding such a machine, it would be as useless as a first-rate man-of-war manned by Oxford clergymen or Parisian shopkeepers. I do not say this to the disparagement of English officers: they have had no means of acquiring experience; but I do say it to create alarm; for we do not appear to me to be half alarmed enough, or to entertain that sense of our danger which leads to the most obvious means of self-defence. As for the spirit of the peasantry in making a gallant defence behind hedge-rows, and through plate-racks and hen-coops, highly as I think of their bravery, I do not know any nation in Europe so likely to be struck with the panic as the English; and this from their total unacquaintance with the science of war. Old wheat and beans blazing for twenty miles round; cart mares shot; sows of Lord Somerville's breed running wild over the country; the minister of the parish wounded sorely in his hinder parts; Mrs. Plymley in fits. All these scenes of war an Austrian or a Russian has seen three or four times over: but it is now three centuries since an English pig has fallen in a fair battle upon English ground, or a farm-house been rifled, or a clergyman's wife been subjected to any other proposals of love than the connubial endearments of her sleek and orthodox mate. The old edition of Plutarch's Lives, which lies in the corner of your parlour window, has contributed to work you up to the most romantic expectations of our Roman behaviour. You are persuaded that Lord Amherst will defend Kew Bridge like Cocles; that some maid of honour will break away from her captivity, and swim over the Thames; that the Duke of York will burn his capitulating hand; and little Mr. Sturges Bourne give forty years' purchase for Moulsham Hall, while the French are encamped upon it. I hope we shall witness all this, if the French do come; but in the meantime I am so enchanted with the ordinary English behaviour of these invaluable persons, that I earnestly pray no opportunity may be given them for Roman valour, and for those very un-Roman pensions which they would all, of course, take especial care to claim in consequence. But whatever was our conduct, if every ploughman was as great a hero as he who was called from his oxen to save Rome from her enemies, I should still say, that at such a crisis you want the affections of all your subjects in both islands: there is no spirit which you must alienate, no art you must avert, every man must feel he has a country, and that there is an urgent and pressing cause why he should expose himself to death.

The effects of penal laws in matters of religion are never confined to those limits in which the legislature intended they should be placed: it is not only that I am excluded from certain offices and dignities because I am a Catholic, but the exclusion carries with it a certain stigma, which degrades me in the eyes of the monopolising sect, and the very name of my religion becomes odious. These effects are so very striking in England, that I solemnly believe blue and red baboons to be more popular here than Catholics and Presbyterians; they are more understood, and there is a greater disposition to do something for them. When a country squire hears of an ape, his first feeling is to give it nuts and apples; when he hears of a Dissenter, his immediate impulse is to commit it to the county gaol, to shave its head, to alter its customary food, and to have it privately whipped. This is no caricature, but an accurate picture of national feelings, as they degrade and endanger us at this very moment. The Irish Catholic gentleman would bear his legal disabilities with greater temper, if these were all he had to bear— if they did not enable every Protestant cheese-monger and tide- waiter to treat him with contempt. He is branded on the forehead with a red-hot iron, and treated like a spiritual felon, because in the highest of all considerations he is led by the noblest of all guides, his own disinterested conscience.

Why are nonsense and cruelty a bit the better because they are enacted? If Providence, which gives wine and oil, had blessed us with that tolerant spirit which makes the countenance more pleasant and the heart more glad than these can do; if our Statute Book had never been defiled with such infamous laws, the sepulchral Spencer Perceval would have been hauled through the dirtiest horse-pond in Hampstead, had he ventured to propose them. But now persecution is good, because it exists; every law which originated in ignorance and malice, and gratifies the passions from whence it sprang, we call the wisdom of our ancestors: when such laws are repealed, they will be cruelty and madness; till they are repealed, they are policy and caution.

I was somewhat amused with the imputation brought against the Catholics by the University of Oxford, that they are enemies to liberty. I immediately turned to my "History of England," and marked as an historical error that passage in which it is recorded that, in the reign of Queen Anne, the famous degree of the University of Oxford respecting passive obedience, was ordered by the House of Lords to be burnt by the hands of the common hangman, as contrary to the liberty of the subject and the law of the land. Nevertheless, I wish, whatever be the modesty of those who impute, that the imputation was a little more true, the Catholic cause would not be quite so desperate with the present. Administration. I fear, however, that the hatred to liberty in these poor devoted wretches may ere long appear more doubtful than it is at present to the Vice-Chancellor and his Clergy, inflamed as they doubtless are with classical examples of republican virtue, and panting, as they always have been, to reduce the power of the Crown within narrower and safer limits. What mistaken zeal to attempt to connect one religion with freedom and another with slavery! Who laid the foundations of English liberty? What was the mixed religion of Switzerland? What has the Protestant religion done for liberty in Denmark, in Sweden, throughout the north of Germany, and in Prussia? The purest religion in the world, in my humble opinion, is the religion of the Church of England: for its preservation (so far as it is exercised without intruding upon the liberties of others) I am ready at this moment to venture my present life, and but through that religion I have no hopes of any other; yet I am not forced to be silly because I am pious; nor will I ever join in eulogiums on my faith which every man of common reading and common sense can so easily refute.

You have either done too much for the Catholics, worthy Abraham, or too little; if you had intended to refuse them political power, you should have refused them civil rights. After you had enabled them to acquire property, after you had conceded to them all that you did concede in '78 and '93, the rest is wholly out of your power: you may choose whether you will give the rest in an honourable or a disgraceful mode, but it is utterly out of your power to withhold it.

In the last year, land to the amount of EIGHT HUNDRED THOUSAND POUNDS was purchased by the Catholics in Ireland. Do you think it possible to be-Perceval, and be-Canning, and be-Castlereagh, such a body of men as this out of their common rights, and their common sense? Mr. George Canning may laugh and joke at the idea of Protestant bailiffs ravishing Catholic ladies, under the 9th clause of the Sunset Bill; but if some better remedy be not applied to the distractions of Ireland than the jocularity of Mr. Canning, they will soon put an end to his pension, and to the pension of those "near and dear relatives," for whose eating, drinking, washing, and clothing, every man in the United Kingdoms now pays his two-pence or three-pence a year. You may call these observations coarse, if you please; but I have no idea that the Sophias and Carolines of any man breathing are to eat national veal, to drink public tea, to wear Treasury ribands, and then that we are to be told that it is coarse to animadvert upon this pitiful and eleemosynary splendour. If this is right, why not mention it? If it is wrong, why should not he who enjoys the ease of supporting his sisters in this manner bear the shame of it? Everybody seems hitherto to have spared a man who never spares anybody.

As for the enormous wax candles, and superstitious mummeries, and painted jackets of the Catholic priests, I fear them not. Tell me that the world will return again under the influence of the smallpox; that Lord Castlereagh will hereafter oppose the power of the Court; that Lord Howick and Mr. Grattan will do each of them a mean and dishonourable action; that anybody who has heard Lord Redesdale speak once will knowingly and willingly hear him again; that Lord Eldon has assented to the fact of two and two making four, without shedding tears, or expressing the smallest doubt or scruple; tell me any other thing absurd or incredible, but, for the love of common sense, let me hear no more of the danger to be apprehended from the general diffusion of Popery. It is too absurd to be reasoned upon; every man feels it is nonsense when he hears it stated, and so does every man while he is stating it.

I cannot imagine why the friends to the Church Establishment should enter in such a horror of seeing the doors of Parliament flung open to the Catholics, and view so passively the enjoyment of that right by the Presbyterians and by every other species of Dissenter. In their tenets, in their Church Government, in the nature of their endowments, the Dissenters are infinitely more distant from the Church of England than the Catholics are; yet the Dissenters have never been excluded from Parliament. There are 45 members in one House, and 16 in the other, who always are Dissenters. There is no law which would prevent every member of the Lords and Commons from being Dissenters. The Catholics could not bring into Parliament half the number of the Scotch members; and yet one exclusion is of such immense importance, because it has taken place; and the other no human being thinks of, because no one is accustomed to it. I have often thought, if the WISDOM OF OUR ANCESTORS had excluded all persons with red hair from the House of Commons, of the throes and convulsions it would occasion to restore them to their natural rights. What mobs and riots would it produce! To what infinite abuse and obloquy would the capillary patriot be exposed; what wormwood would distil from Mr. Perceval, what froth would drop from Mr. Canning; how (I will not say MY, but OUR Lord Hawkesbury, for he belongs to us all)— how our Lord Hawkesbury would work away about the hair of King William and Lord Somers, and the authors of the great and glorious Revolution; how Lord Eldon would appeal to the Deity and his own virtues, and to the hair of his children: some would say that red-haired men were superstitious; some would prove they were atheists; they would be petitioned against as the friends of slavery, and the advocates for revolt; in short, such a corruptor of the heart and understanding is the spirit of persecution, that these unfortunate people (conspired against by their fellow-subjects of every complexion), if they did not emigrate to countries where hair of another colour was persecuted, would be driven to the falsehood of perukes, or the hypocrisy of the Tricosian fluid.

As for the dangers of the Church (in spite of the staggering events which have lately taken place), I have not yet entirely lost my confidence in the power of common sense, and I believe the Church to be in no danger at all; but if it is, that danger is not from the Catholics, but from the Methodists, and from that patent Christianity which has been for some time manufacturing at Clapham, to the prejudice of the old and admirable article prepared by the Church. I would counsel my lords the Bishops to keep their eyes upon that holy village, and its vicinity; they will find there a zeal in making converts far superior to anything which exists among the Catholics; a contempt for the great mass of English clergy, much more rooted and profound; and a regular fund to purchase livings for those groaning and garrulous gentlemen whom they denominate (by a standing sarcasm against the regular Church) Gospel preachers and vital clergymen. I am too firm a believer in the general propriety and respectability of the English clergy, to believe they have much to fear either from old nonsense or from new; but if the Church must be supposed to be in danger, I prefer that nonsense which is grown half venerable from time, the force of which I have already tried and baffled, which at least has some excuse in the dark and ignorant ages in which it originated. The religious enthusiasm manufactured by living men before my own eyes disgusts my understanding as much, influences my imagination not at all, and excites my apprehensions much more.

I may have seemed to you to treat the situation of public affairs with some degree of levity; but I feel it deeply, and with nightly and daily anguish; because I know Ireland; I have known it all my life; I love it, and I foresee the crisis to which it will soon be exposed. Who can doubt but that Ireland will experience ultimately from France a treatment to which the conduct they have experienced from England is the love of a parent, or a brother? Who can doubt but that five years after he has got hold of the country, Ireland will be tossed away by Bonaparte as a present to some one of his ruffian generals, who will knock the head of Mr. Keogh against the head of Cardinal Troy, shoot twenty of the most noisy blockheads of the Roman persuasion, wash his pug-dogs in holy water, and confiscate the salt butter of the Milesian republic to the last tub? But what matters this? or who is wise enough in Ireland to heed it? or when had common sense much influence with my poor dear Irish? Mr. Perceval does not know the Irish; but I know them, and I know that at every rash and mad hazard they will break the Union, revenge their wounded pride and their insulted religion, and fling themselves into the open arms of France, sure of dying in the embrace. And now, what means have you of guarding against this coming evil, upon which the future happiness or misery of every Englishman depends? Have you a single ally in the whole world? Is there a vulnerable point in the French empire where the astonishing resources of that people can be attracted and employed? Have you a ministry wise enough to comprehend the danger, manly enough to believe unpleasant intelligence, honest enough to state their apprehensions at the peril of their places? Is there anywhere the slightest disposition to join any measure of love, or conciliation, or hope, with that dreadful bill which the distractions of Ireland have rendered necessary? At the very moment that the last Monarchy in Europe has fallen, are we not governed by a man of pleasantry, and a man of theology? In the six hundredth year of our empire over Ireland, have we any memorial of ancient kindness to refer to? any people, any zeal, any country on which we can depend? Have we any hope, but in the winds of heaven and the tides of the sea? any prayer to prefer to the Irish, but that they should forget and forgive their oppressors, who, in the very moment that they are calling upon them for their exertions, solemnly assure them that the oppression shall still remain?

Abraham, farewell! If I have tired you, remember how often you have tired me and others. I do not think we really differ in politics so much as you suppose; or at least, if we do, that difference is in the means, and not in the end. We both love the Constitution, respect the King, and abhor the French. But though you love the Constitution, you would perpetuate the abuses which have been engrafted upon it; though you respect the King, you would confirm his scruples against the Catholics; though you abhor the French, you would open to them the conquest of Ireland. My method of respecting my sovereign is by protecting his honour, his empire, and his lasting happiness; I evince my love of the Constitution by making it the guardian of all men's rights and the source of their freedom; and I prove my abhorrence of the French, by uniting against them the disciples of every church in the only remaining nation in Europe. As for the men of whom I have been compelled in this age of mediocrity to say so much, they cannot of themselves be worth a moment's consideration, to you, to me, or to anybody. In a year after their death they will be forgotten as completely as if they had never been; and are now of no further importance than as they are the mere vehicles of carrying into effect the common-place and mischievous prejudices of the times in which they live.

LETTER VI.

Dear Abraham,—What amuses me the most is to hear of the INDULGENCES which the Catholics have received, and their exorbitance in not being satisfied with those indulgences: now if you complain to me that a man is obtrusive and shameless in his requests, and that it is impossible to bring him to reason, I must first of all hear the whole of your conduct towards him; for you may have taken from him so much in the first instance that, in spite of a long series of restitution, a vast latitude for petition may still remain behind.

There is a village, no matter where, in which the inhabitants, on one day in the year, sit down to a dinner prepared at the common expense: by an extra-ordinary piece of tyranny, which Lord Hawkesbury would call the wisdom of the village ancestors, the inhabitants of three of the streets, about a hundred years ago, seized upon the inhabitants of the fourth street, bound them hand and foot, laid them upon their backs, and compelled them to look on while the rest were stuffing themselves with beef and beer; the next year the inhabitants of the persecuted street, though they contributed an equal quota of the expense, were treated precisely in the same manner. The tyranny grew into a custom; and, as the manner of our nature is, it was considered as the most sacred of all duties to keep these poor fellows without their annual dinner. The village was so tenacious of this practice, that nothing could induce them to resign it; every enemy to it was looked upon as a disbeliever in Divine Providence, and any nefarious churchwarden who wished to succeed in his election had nothing to do but to represent his antagonist as an abolitionist, in order to frustrate his ambition, endanger his life, and throw the village into a state of the most dreadful commotion. By degrees, however, the obnoxious street grew to be so well peopled, and its inhabitants so firmly united, that their oppressors, more afraid of injustice, were more disposed to be just. At the next dinner they are unbound, the year after allowed to sit upright, then a bit of bread and a glass of water; till at last, after a long series of concessions, they are emboldened to ask, in pretty plain terms, that they may be allowed to sit down at the bottom of the table, and to fill their bellies as well as the rest. Forthwith a general cry of shame and scandal: "Ten years ago, were you not laid upon your backs? Don't you remember what a great thing you thought it to get a piece of bread? How thankful you were for cheese parings? Have you forgotten that memorable era, when the lord of the manor interfered to obtain for you a slice of the public pudding? And now, with an audacity only equalled by your ingratitude, you have the impudence to ask for knives and forks, and to request, in terms too plain to be mistaken, that you may sit down to table with the rest, and be indulged even with beef and beer: there are not more than half a dozen dishes which we have reserved for ourselves; the rest has been thrown open to you in the utmost profusion; you have potatoes, and carrots, suet dumplings, sops in the pan, and delicious toast and water in incredible quantities. Beef, mutton, lamb, pork, and veal are ours; and if you were not the most restless and dissatisfied of human beings, you would never think of aspiring to enjoy them."

Is not this, my dainty Abraham, the very nonsense and the very insult which is talked to and practised upon the Catholics? You are surprised that men who have tasted of partial justice should ask for perfect justice; that he who has been robbed of coat and cloak will not be contented with the restitution of one of his garments. He would be a very lazy blockhead if he were content, and I (who, though an inhabitant of the village, have preserved, thank God, some sense of justice) most earnestly counsel these half-fed claimants to persevere in their just demands, till they are admitted to a more complete share of a dinner for which they pay as much as the others; and if they see a little attenuated lawyer squabbling at the head of their opponents, let them desire him to empty his pockets, and to pull out all the pieces of duck, fowl, and pudding which he has filched from the public feast, to carry home to his wife and children.

You parade a great deal upon the vast concessions made by this country to the Irish before the Union. I deny that any voluntary concession was ever made by England to Ireland. What did Ireland ever ask that was granted? What did she ever demand that was not refused? How did she get her Mutiny Bill—a limited Parliament—a repeal of Poyning's Law—a constitution? Not by the concessions of England, but by her fears. When Ireland asked for all these things upon her knees, her petitions were rejected with Percevalism and contempt; when she demanded them with the voice of 60,000 armed men, they were granted with every mark of consternation and dismay. Ask of Lord Auckland the fatal consequences of trifling with such a people as the Irish. He himself was the organ of these refusals. As secretary to the Lord Lieutenant, the insolence and the tyranny of this country passed through his hands. Ask him if he remembers the consequences. Ask him if he has forgotten that memorable evening when he came down booted and mantled to the House of Commons, when he told the House he was about to set off for Ireland that night, and declared before God, if he did not carry with him a compliance with all their demands, Ireland was for ever lost to this country. The present generation have forgotten this; but I have not forgotten it; and I know, hasty and undignified as the submission of England then was, that

Lord Auckland was right, that the delay of a single day might very probably have separated the two peoples for ever. The terms submission and fear are galling terms when applied from the lesser nation to the greater; but it is the plain historical truth, it is the natural consequence of injustice, it is the predicament in which every country places itself which leaves such a mass of hatred and discontent by its side. No empire is powerful enough to endure it; it would exhaust the strength of China, and sink it with all its mandarins and tea-kettles to the bottom of the deep. By refusing them justice now when you are strong enough to refuse them anything more than justice, you will act over again, with the Catholics, the same scene of mean and precipitate submission which disgraced you before America, and before the volunteers of Ireland. We shall live to hear the Hampstead Protestant pronouncing such extravagant panegyrics upon holy water, and paying such fulsome compliments to the thumbs and offals of departed saints, that parties will change sentiments, and Lord Henry Petty and Sam Whitbread take a spell at No Popery. The wisdom of Mr. Fox was alike employed in teaching his country justice when Ireland was weak, and dignity when Ireland was strong. We are fast pacing round the same miserable circle of ruin and imbecility. Alas! where is our guide?

You say that Ireland is a millstone about our necks; that it would be better for us if Ireland were sunk at the bottom of the sea; that the Irish are a nation of irreclaimable savages and barbarians. How often have I heard these sentiments fall from the plump and thoughtless squire, and from the thriving English shopkeeper, who has never felt the rod of an Orange master upon his back. Ireland a millstone about your neck! Why is it not a stone of Ajax in your hand? I agree with you most cordially that, governed as Ireland now is, it would be a vast accession of strength if the waves of the sea were to rise and engulf her to-morrow. At this moment, opposed as we are to all the world, the annihilation of one of the most fertile islands on the face of the globe, containing five millions of human creatures, would be one of the most solid advantages which could happen to this country. I doubt very much, in spite of all the just abuse which has been lavished upon Bonaparte, whether there is any one of his conquered countries the blotting out of which would be as beneficial to him as the destruction of Ireland would be to us: of countries I speak differing in language from the French, little habituated to their intercourse, and inflamed with all the resentments of a recently-conquered people. Why will you attribute the turbulence of our people to any cause but the right—to any cause but your own scandalous oppression? If you tie your horse up to a gate, and beat him cruelly, is he vicious because he kicks you? If you have plagued and worried a mastiff dog for years, is he mad because he flies at you whenever he sees you? Hatred is an active, troublesome passion. Depend upon it, whole nations have always some reason for their hatred. Before you refer the turbulence of the Irish to incurable defects in their character, tell me if you have treated them as friends and equals? Have you protected their commerce? Have you respected their religion? Have you been as anxious for their freedom as your own? Nothing of all this. What then? Why you have confiscated the territorial surface of the country twice over: you have massacred and exported her inhabitants: you have deprived four-fifths of them of every civil privilege: you have at every period made her commerce and manufactures slavishly subordinate to your own: and yet the hatred which the Irish bear to you is the result of an original turbulence of character, and of a primitive, obdurate wildness, utterly incapable of civilisation. The embroidered inanities and the sixth- form effusions of Mr. Canning are really not powerful enough to make me believe this; nor is there any authority on earth (always excepting the Dean of Christ Church) which could make it credible to me. I am sick of Mr. Canning. There is not a "ha'porth of bread to all this sugar and sack." I love not the cretaceous and incredible countenance of his colleague. The only opinion in which I agree with these two gentlemen is that which they entertain of each other. I am sure that the insolence of Mr. Pitt, and the unbalanced accounts of Melville, were far better than the perils of this new ignorance:-

Nonne   fuit   satius,   ristes   Amaryllidis   iras
Atque   superba   pati   fastidia?   nonne   Menalcan?
Quamvis ille niger?

In the midst of the most profound peace, the secret
articles of the Treaty of Tilsit, in which the destruction of
Ireland is resolved upon, induce you to rob the Danes of
their fleet. After the expedition sailed comes the Treaty of
Tilsit, containing no article, public or private, alluding to
Ireland. The state of the world, you tell me, justified us in
doing this. Just God! do we think only of the state of the
world when there is an opportunity for robbery, for murder,
and for plunder; and do we forget the state of the world when
we are called upon to be wise, and good, and just? Does the
state of the world never remind us that we have four millions
of subjects whose injuries we ought to atone for, and whose
affections we ought to conciliate? Does the state of the world
never warn us to lay aside our infernal bigotry, and to arm
every man who acknowledges a God, and can grasp a sword?
Did it never occur to this administration that they might
virtuously get hold of a force ten times greater than the force
of the Danish fleet? Was there no other way of protecting
Ireland but by bringing eternal shame upon Great Britain,
and by making the earth a den of robbers? See what the
men whom you have supplanted would have done. They
would have rendered the invasion of Ireland impossible, by
restoring to the Catholics their long-lost rights: they would

have acted in such a manner that the French would neither have wished for invasion nor dared to attempt it: they would have increased the permanent strength of the country while they preserved its reputation unsullied. Nothing of this kind your friends have done, because they are solemnly pledged to do nothing of this kind; because, to tolerate all religions, and to equalise civil rights to all sects, is to oppose some of the worst passions of our nature—to plunder and to oppress is to gratify them all. They wanted the huzzas of mobs, and they have for ever blasted the fame of England to obtain them. Were the fleets of Holland, France, and Spain destroyed by larceny? You resisted the power of 150 sail of the line by sheer courage, and violated every principle of morals from the dread of fifteen hulks, while the expedition itself cost you three times more than the value of the larcenous matter brought away. The French trample on the laws of God and man, not for old cordage, but for kingdoms, and always take care to be well paid for their crimes. We contrive, under the present administration, to unite moral with intellectual deficiency, and to grow weaker and worse by the same action. If they had any evidence of the intended hostility of the Danes, why was it not produced? Why have the nations of Europe been allowed to feel an indignation against this country beyond the reach of all subsequent information? Are these times, do you imagine, when we can trifle with a year of universal hatred, dally with the curses of Europe, and then regain a lost character at pleasure, by the parliamentary perspirations of the Foreign Secretary, or the solemn asseverations of the pecuniary Rose? Believe me, Abraham, it is not under such ministers as these that the dexterity of honest Englishmen will ever equal the dexterity of French knaves; it is not in their presence that the serpent of Moses will ever swallow up the serpents of the magician.

Lord Hawkesbury says that nothing is to be granted to the Catholics from fear. What! not even justice? Why not? There are four millions of disaffected people within twenty miles of your own coast. I fairly confess that the dread which I have of their physical power is with me a very strong motive for listening to their claims. To talk of not acting from fear, is mere parliamentary cant. From what motive but fear, I should be glad to know, have all the improvements in our constitution proceeded? I question if any justice has ever been done to large masses of mankind from any other motive. By what other motives can the plunderers of the Baltic suppose nations to be governed in their intercourse WITH EACH OTHER? If I say, Give this people what they ask because it is just, do you think I should get ten people to listen to me? Would not the lesser of the two Jenkinsons be the first to treat me with contempt? The only true way to make the mass of mankind see the beauty of justice is by showing to them, in pretty plain terms, the consequences of injustice. If any body of French troops land in Ireland, the whole population of that country will rise against you to a man, and you could not possibly survive such an event three years. Such, from the bottom of my soul, do I believe to be the present state of that country; and so far does it appear to me to be impolitic and unstatesman-like to concede anything to such a danger, that if the Catholics, in addition to their present just demands, were to petition for the perpetual removal of the said Lord Hawkesbury from his Majesty's councils, I think, whatever might be the effect upon the destinies of Europe, and however it might retard our own individual destruction, that the prayer of the petition should be instantly complied with. Canning's crocodile tears should not move me; the hoops of the maids of honour should not hide him. I would tear him from the banisters of the back stairs, and plunge him in the fishy fumes of the dirtiest of all his Cinque Ports.

LETTER VII.

Dear Abraham,—In the correspondence which is passing between us, you are perpetually alluding to the Foreign Secretary; and in answer to the dangers of Ireland, which I am pressing upon your notice, you have nothing to urge but the confidence which you repose in the discretion and sound sense of this gentleman. I can only say, that I have

listened to him long and often with the greatest attention; I
have used every exertion in my power to take a fair measure
of him, and it appears to me impossible to hear him upon
any arduous topic without perceiving that he is eminently
deficient in those solid and serious qualities upon which,
and upon which alone, the confidence of a great country
can properly repose. He sweats and labours, and works for
sense, and Mr. Ellis seems always to think it is coming, but
it does not come; the machine can't draw up what is not to
be found in the spring; Providence has made him a light,
jesting, paragraph-writing man, and that he will remain
to his dying day. When he is jocular he is strong, when he
is serious he is like Samson in a wig; any ordinary person
is a match for him: a song, an ironical letter, a burlesque
ode, an attack in the newspaper upon Nicoll's eye, a smart
speech of twenty minutes, full of gross misrepresentations
and clever turns, excellent language, a spirited manner,
lucky quotation, success in provoking dull men, some half
information picked up in Pall Mall in the morning; these
are your friend's natural weapons; all these things he can do:
here I allow him to be truly great; nay, I will be just, and
go still further, if he would confine himself to these things,
and consider the facete and the playful to be the basis of his
character, he would, for that species of man, be universally
regarded as a person of a very good understanding; call him
a legislator, a reasoner, and the conductor of the affairs of a

great nation, and it seems to me as absurd as if a butterfly were to teach bees to make honey. That he is an extraordinary writer of small poetry, and a diner out of the highest lustre, I do most readily admit. After George Selwyn, and perhaps Tickell, there has been no such man for this half-century. The Foreign Secretary is a gentleman, a respectable as well as a highly agreeable man in private life; but you may as well feed me with decayed potatoes as console me for the miseries of Ireland by the resources of his SENSE and his DISCRETION. It is only the public situation which this gentleman holds which entitles me or induces me to say so much about him. He is a fly in amber, nobody cares about the fly; the only question is, How the devil did it get there ? Nor do I attack him for the love of glory, but from the love of utility, as a burgomaster hunts a rat in a Dutch dyke, for fear it should flood a province.

The friends of the Catholic question are, I observe, extremely embarrassed in arguing when they come to the loyalty of the Irish Catholics. As for me, I shall go straight forward to my object, and state what I have no manner of doubt, from an intimate knowledge of Ireland, to be the plain truth. Of the great Roman Catholic proprietors, and of the Catholic prelates, there may be a few, and but a few, who would follow the fortunes of England at all events: there is another set of men who, thoroughly detesting this country, have too much property and too much character to lose, not to wait for some very favourable event before they show themselves; but the great mass of Catholic population, upon the slightest appearance of a French force in that country, would rise upon you to a man. It is the most mistaken policy to conceal the plain truth. There is no loyalty among the Catholics: they detest you as their worst oppressors, and they will continue to detest you till you remove the cause of their hatred. It is in your power in six months' time to produce a total revolution of opinions among this people; and in some future letter I will show you that this is clearly the case. At present, see what a dreadful in state Ireland is in. The common toast among the low Irish is, the feast of the PASSOVER. Some allusion to Bonaparte, in a play lately acted at Dublin, produced thunders of applause from the pit and the galleries; and a politician should not be inattentive to the public feelings expressed in theatres. Mr. Perceval thinks he has disarmed the Irish: he has no more disarmed the Irish than he has resigned a shilling of his own public emoluments. An Irish peasant fills the barrel of his gun full of tow dipped in oil, butters up the lock, buries it in a bog, and allows the Orange bloodhound to ransack his cottage at pleasure. Be just and kind to the Irish, and you will indeed disarm them; rescue them from the degraded servitude in which they are held by a handful of their own countrymen, and you will add four millions of brave and affectionate men to your strength. Nightly visits, Protestant inspectors, licenses to possess a pistol, or a knife and fork, the odious vigour of the EVANGELICAL Perceval— acts of Parliament, drawn up by some English attorney, to save you from the hatred of four millions of people—the guarding yourselves from universal disaffection by a police; a confidence in the little cunning of Bow Street, when you might rest your security upon the eternal basis of the best feelings: this is the meanness and madness to which nations are reduced when they lose sight of the first elements of justice, without which a country can be no more secure than it can be healthy without air. I sicken at such policy and such men. The fact is, the Ministers know nothing about the present state of Ireland; Mr. Perceval sees a few clergymen, Lord Castlereagh a few general officers, who take care, of course, to report what is pleasant rather than what is true. As for the joyous and lepid consul, he jokes upon neutral flags and frauds, jokes upon Irish rebels, jokes upon northern and western and southern foes, and gives himself no trouble upon any subject; nor is the mediocrity of the idolatrous deputy of the slightest use. Dissolved in grins, he reads no memorials upon the state of Ireland, listens to no reports, asks no questions, and is the

"BOURN from whom no traveller returns."

The danger of an immediate insurrection is now, I BELIEVE, blown over. You have so strong an army in Ireland, and the Irish are become so much more cunning from the last insurrection, that you may perhaps be tolerably secure just at present from that evil: but are you secure from the efforts which the French may make to throw a body of troops into Ireland? and do you consider that event to be difficult and improbable? From Brest Harbour to Cape St. Vincent, you have above three thousand miles of hostile sea coast, and twelve or fourteen harbours quite capable of containing a sufficient force for the powerful invasion of Ireland. The nearest of these harbours is not two days' sail from the southern coast of Ireland, with a fair leading wind; and the furthest not ten. Five ships of the line, for so very short a passage, might carry five or six thousand troops with cannon and ammunition; and Ireland presents to their attack a southern coast of more than 500 miles, abounding in deep bays, admirable harbours, and disaffected inhabitants. Your blockading ships may be forced to come home for provisions and repairs, or they may be blown off in a gale of wind and compelled to bear away for their own coast; and you will observe that the very same wind which locks you up in the British Channel, when you are got there, is evidently favourable for the invasion of Ireland. And yet this is called Government, and the people huzza Mr. Perceval for continuing to expose his country day after day to such tremendous perils as these; cursing the men who would have given up a question in theology to have saved us from such a risk. The British empire at this moment is in the state of a peach-blossom—if the wind blows gently from one quarter, it survives; if furiously from the other, it perishes. A stiff breeze may set in from the north, the Rochefort squadron will be taken, and the Minister will be the most holy of men: if it comes from some other point, Ireland is gone; we curse ourselves as a set of monastic madmen, and call out for the unavailing satisfaction of Mr. Perceval's head. Such a state of political existence is scarcely credible: it is the action of a mad young fool standing upon one foot, and peeping down the crater of Mount AEtna, not the conduct of a wise and sober people deciding upon their best and dearest interests: and in the name, the much- injured name, of heaven, what is it all for that we expose ourselves to these dangers? Is it that we may sell more muslin? Is it that we may acquire more territory? Is it that we may strengthen what we have already acquired? No; nothing of all this; but that one set of Irishmen may torture another set of Irishmen—that Sir Phelim O'Callaghan may continue to whip Sir Toby M'Tackle, his next door neighbour, and continue to ravish his Catholic daughters; and these are the measures which the honest and consistent Secretary supports; and this is the Secretary whose genius in the estimation of Brother Abraham is to extinguish the genius of Bonaparte. Pompey was killed by a slave, Goliath smitten by a stripling, Pyrrhus died by the hand of a woman; tremble, thou great Gaul, from whose head an armed Minerva leaps forth in the hour of danger; tremble, thou scourge of God, a pleasant man is come out against thee, and thou shalt be laid low by a joker of jokes, and he shall talk his pleasant talk against thee, and thou shalt be no more!

You tell me, in spite of all this parade of sea-coast, Bonaparte has neither ships nor sailors: but this is a mistake. He has not ships and sailors to contest the empire of the seas with Great Britain, but there remains quite sufficient of the navies of France, Spain, Holland, and Denmark, for these short excursions and invasions. Do you think, too, that Bonaparte does not add to his navy every year? Do you suppose, with all Europe at his feet, that he can find any difficulty in obtaining timber, and that money will not procure for him any quantity of naval stores he may want? The mere machine, the empty ship, he can build as well, and as quickly, as you can; and though he may not find enough of practised sailors to man large fighting-fleets—it is not possible to conceive that he can want sailors for such sort of purposes as I have stated. He is at present the despotic monarch of above twenty thousand miles of sea- coast, and yet you suppose he cannot procure sailors for the invasion of Ireland. Believe, if you please, that such a fleet met at sea by any number of our ships at all comparable to them in point of force, would be immediately taken, let it be so; I count nothing upon their power of resistance, only upon their power of escaping unobserved. If experience has taught us anything, it is the impossibility of perpetual blockades. The instances are innumerable, during the course of this war, where whole fleets have sailed in and out of harbour, in spite of every vigilance used to prevent it. I shall only mention those cases where Ireland is concerned. In December, 1796, seven ships of the line, and ten transports, reached Bantry Bay from Brest, without having seen an English ship in their passage. It blew a storm when they were off shore, and therefore England still continues to be an independent kingdom. You will observe that at the very time the French fleet sailed out of Brest Harbour, Admiral Colpoys was cruising off there with a powerful squadron, and still, from the particular circumstances of the weather, found it impossible to prevent the French from coming out. During the time that Admiral Colpoys was cruising off Brest, Admiral Richery, with six ships of the line, passed him, and got safe into the harbour. At the very moment when the French squadron was lying in Bantry Bay, Lord Bridport with his fleet was locked up by a foul wind in the Channel, and for several days could not stir to the assistance of Ireland. Admiral Colpoys, totally unable to find the French fleet, came home. Lord Bridport, at the change of the wind, cruised for them in vain, and they got safe back to Brest, without having seen a single one of those floating bulwarks, the possession of which we believe will enable us with impunity to set justice and common sense at defiance.

Such is the miserable and precarious state of an anemocracy, of a people who put their trust in hurricanes, and are governed by wind. In August, 1798, three forty-gun frigates landed 1,100 men under Humbert, making the passage from Rochelle to Killala without seeing any English ship. In October of the same year, four French frigates anchored in Killala Bay with 2,000 troops; and though they did not land their troops, they returned to France in safety. In the same month, a line-of-battle ship, eight stout frigates, and a brig, all full of troops and stores, reached the coast of Ireland, and were fortunately, in sight of land, destroyed, after an obstinate engagement, by Sir John Warren.

If you despise the little troop which, in these numerous experiments, did make good its landing, take with you, if you please, this precis of its exploits: eleven hundred men, commanded by a soldier raised from the ranks, put to rout a select army of 6,000 men, commanded by General Lake, seized their ordnance, ammunition, and stores, advanced 150 miles into a country containing an armed force of 150,000 men, and at last surrendered to the Viceroy, an experienced general, gravely and cautiously advancing at the head of all his chivalry and of an immense army to oppose him. You must excuse these details about Ireland, but it appears to me to be of all other subjects the most important. If we conciliate Ireland, we can do nothing amiss; if we do not, we can do nothing well. If Ireland was friendly, we might equally set at defiance the talents of Bonaparte and the blunders of his rival, Mr. Canning; we could then support the ruinous and silly bustle of our useless expeditions, and the almost incredible ignorance of our commercial orders in council. Let the present administration give up but this one point, and there is nothing which I would not consent to grant them. Mr. Perceval shall have full liberty to insult the tomb of Mr. Fox, and to torment every eminent Dissenter in Great Britain; Lord Camden shall have large boxes of plums; Mr. Rose receive permission to prefix to his name the appellative of virtuous; and to the Viscount Castlereagh a round sum of ready money shall be well and truly paid into his hand. Lastly, what remains to Mr. George Canning, but that he ride up and down Pall Mall glorious upon a white horse, and that they cry out before him, Thus shall it be done to the statesman who hath written "The Needy Knife-Grinder," and the German play? Adieu only for the present; you shall soon hear from me again; it is a subject upon which I cannot long be silent.

LETTER VIII.

Nothing can be more erroneous than to suppose that Ireland is not bigger than the Isle of Wight, or of more consequence than Guernsey or Jersey; and yet I am almost inclined to believe, from the general supineness which prevails here respecting the dangerous state of that country, that such is the rank which it holds in our statistical tables. I have been writing to you a great deal about Ireland, and perhaps it may be of some use to state to you concisely the nature and resources of the country which has been the subject of our long and strange correspondence. There were returned, as I have before observed, to the hearth tax in 1791, 701,102 houses, which Mr. Newenham shows from unquestionable documents to be nearly 80,000 below the real number of houses in that country. There are 27,457 square English miles in Ireland, and more than five millions of people.

By the last survey it appears that the inhabited houses in England and Wales amount to 1,574,902, and the population to 9,343,578, which gives an average of 5.875 to each house, in a country where the density of population is certainly less considerable than in Ireland. It is commonly supposed that two-fifths of the army and navy are Irishmen, at periods when political disaffection does not avert the Catholics from the service. The current value of Irish exports in 1807 was 9,314,854 pounds 17s. 7d.; a state of commerce about equal to the commerce of England in the middle of the reign of George II. The tonnage of ships entered inward and cleared outward in the trade of Ireland, in 1807, amounted to 1,567,430 tons. The quantity of home spirits exported amounted to 10,284 gallons in 1796, and to 930,800 gallons in 1804. Of the exports which I have stated, provisions amounted to four millions, and linen to about four millions and a half. There was exported from Ireland, upon an average of two years ending in January, 1804, 591,274 barrels of barley, oats, and wheat; and by weight 910,848 cwts. of flour, oatmeal, barley, oats, and wheat. The amount of butter exported in 1804, from Ireland, was worth, in money, 1,704,680 pounds sterling. The importation of ale and beer, from the immense manufactures now carrying on of these articles, was diminished to 3,209 barrels, in the year 1804, from 111,920 barrels, which was the average importation per annum, taking from three years ending in 1792; and at present there is an export trade of porter. On an average of three years, ending March, 1783, there were imported into Ireland, of cotton wool, 3,326 cwts., of cotton yarn, 5,405 lbs.; but on an average of three years, ending January, 1803, there were imported, of the first article, 13,159 cwts., and of the latter, 628,406 lbs. It is impossible to conceive any manufacture more flourishing. The export of linen has increased in Ireland from 17,776,862 yards, the average in 1770, to 43,534,971 yards, the amount in 1805. The tillage of Ireland has more than trebled within the last twenty-one years. The importation of coals has increased from 230,000 tons in 1783, to 417,030 in 1804; of tobacco, from 3,459,861 lbs. in 1783, to 6,611,543 in 1804; of tea, from 1,703,855 lbs. in 1783, to 3,358,256 in 1804; of sugar, from 143,117 cwts. in 1782, to 309,076 in 1804. Ireland now supports a funded debt of above 64 millions, and it is computed that more than three millions' of money are annually remitted to Irish absentees resident in this country. In Mr. Foster's report, of 100 folio pages, presented to the House of Commons in the year 1806, the total expenditure of Ireland is stated at 9,760,013 pounds. Ireland has increased about two-thirds in its population within twenty-five years, and yet, and in about the same space of time, its exports of beef, bullocks, cows, pork, swine, butter, wheat, barley, and oats, collectively taken, have doubled; and this, in spite of two years' famine, and the presence of an immense army, that is always at hand to guard the most valuable appanage of our empire from joining our most inveterate enemies. Ireland has the greatest possible facilities for carrying on commerce with the whole of Europe. It contains, within a circuit of 750 miles, 66 secure harbours, and presents a western frontier against Great Britain, reaching from the Firth of Clyde north to the Bristol Channel south, and varying in distance from 20 to 100 miles; so that the subjugation of Ireland would compel us to guard with ships and soldiers a new line of coast, certainly amounting, with all its sinuosities, to more than 700 miles—an addition of polemics, in our present state of hostility with all the world, which must highly gratify the vigorists, and give them an ample opportunity of displaying that foolish energy upon which their claims to distinction are founded. Such is the country which the Right Reverend the Chancellor of the Exchequer would drive into the arms of France, and for the conciliation of which we are requested to wait, as if it were one of those sinecure places which were given to Mr. Perceval snarling at the breast, and which cannot be abolished till his decease.

How sincerely and fervently have I often wished that the Emperor of the French had thought as Mr. Spencer Perceval does upon the subject of government; that he had entertained doubts and scruples upon the propriety of admitting the Protestants to an equality of rights with the Catholics, and that he had left in the middle of his empire these vigorous seeds of hatred and disaffection! But the world was never yet conquered by a blockhead. One of the very first measures we saw him recurring to was the complete establishment of religious liberty: if his subjects fought and paid as he pleased, he allowed them to believe as they pleased: the moment I saw this, my best hopes were lost. I perceived in a moment the kind of man we had to do with. I was well aware of the miserable ignorance and folly of this country upon the subject of toleration; and every year has been adding to the success of that game, which it was clear he had the will and the ability to play against us.

You say Bonaparte is not in earnest upon the subject of religion, and that this is the cause of his tolerant spirit;

but is it possible you can intend to give us such dreadful and unamiable notions of religion. Are we to understand that the moment a man is sincere he is narrow-minded; that persecution is the child of belief; and that a desire to leave all men in the quiet and unpunished exercise of their own creed can only exist in the mind of an infidel? Thank God! I know many men whose principles are as firm as they are expanded, who cling tenaciously to their own modification of the Christian faith, without the slightest disposition to force that modification upon other people. If Bonaparte is liberal in subjects of religion because he has no religion, is this a reason why we should be illiberal because we are Christians? If he owes this excellent quality to a vice, is that any reason why we may not owe it to a virtue? Toleration is a great good, and a good to be imitated, let it come from whom it will. If a sceptic is tolerant, it only shows that he is not foolish in practice as well as erroneous in theory. If a religious man is tolerant, it evinces that he is religious from thought and inquiry, because he exhibits in his conduct one of the most beautiful and important consequences of a religious mind—an inviolable charity to all the honest varieties of human opinion.

Lord Sidmouth, and all the anti-Catholic people, little foresee that they will hereafter be the sport of the antiquary; that their prophecies of ruin and destruction from Catholic emancipation will be clapped into the notes of some quaint history, and be matter of pleasantry even to the sedulous housewife and the rural dean. There is always a copious supply of Lord Sidmouths in the world; nor is there one single source of human happiness against which they have not uttered the most lugubrious predictions. Turnpike roads, navigable canals, inoculation, hops, tobacco, the Reformation, the Revolution—there are always a set of worthy and moderately-gifted men, who bawl out death and ruin upon every valuable change which the varying aspect of human affairs absolutely and imperiously requires. I have often thought that it would be extremely useful to make a collection of the hatred and abuse that all those changes have experienced, which are now admitted to be marked improvements in our condition. Such a history might make folly a little more modest, and suspicious of its own decisions.

Ireland, you say, since the Union is to be considered as a part of the whole kingdom; and therefore, however Catholics may predominate in that particular spot, yet, taking the whole empire together, they are to be considered as a much more insignificant quota of the population. Consider them in what light you please, as part of the whole, or by themselves, or in what manner may be most consentaneous to the devices of your holy mind—I say in a very few words, if you do not relieve these people from the civil incapacities to which they are exposed, you will lose them; or you must employ great strength and much treasure in watching over them. In the present state of the world you can afford to do neither the one nor the other. Having stated this, I shall leave you to be ruined, Puffendorf in hand (as Mr. Secretary Canning says), and to lose Ireland, just as you have found out what proportion the aggrieved people should bear to the whole population before their calamities meet with redress. As for your parallel cases, I am no more afraid of deciding upon them than I am upon their prototype. If ever any one heresy should so far spread itself over the principality of Wales that the Established Church were left in a minority of one to four; if you had subjected these heretics to very severe civil privations; if the consequence of such privations were a universal state of disaffection among that caseous and wrathful people; and if at the same time you were at war with all the world, how can you doubt for a moment that I would instantly restore them to a state of the most complete civil liberty? What matters it under what name you put the same case? Common sense is not changed by appellations. I have said how I would act to Ireland, and I would act so to all the world.

I admit that, to a certain degree, the Government will lose the affections of the Orangemen by emancipating the Catholics; much less, however, at present, than three years past. The few men, who have ill-treated the whole crew, live in constant terror that the oppressed people will rise upon them and carry the ship into Brest: —they begin to find that it is a very tiresome thing to sleep every night with cocked pistols under their pillows, and to breakfast, dine, and sup with drawn hangers. They suspect that the privilege of beating and kicking the rest of the sailors is hardly worth all this anxiety, and that if the ship does ever fall into the hands of the disaffected, all the cruelties which they have experienced will be thoroughly remembered and amply repaid. To a short period of disaffection among the Orangemen I confess I should not much object: my love of poetical justice does carry me as far as that; one summer's whipping, only one: the thumb-screw for a short season; a little light easy torturing between Ladyday and Michaelmas; a short specimen of Mr. Perceval's rigour. I have malice enough to ask this slight atonement for the groans and shrieks of the poor Catholics, unheard by any human tribunal, but registered by the Angel of God against their Protestant and enlightened oppressors.

Besides, if you who count ten so often can count five, you must perceive that it is better to have four friends and one enemy than four enemies and one friend; and the more violent the hatred of the Orangemen, the more certain the reconciliation of the Catholics. The disaffection of the Orangemen will be the Irish rainbow: when I see it I shall be sure that the storm is over.

If these incapacities, from which the Catholics ask to be relieved, were to the mass of them only a mere feeling of pride, and if the question were respecting the attainment of privileges which could be of importance only to the highest of the sect, I should still say that the pride of the mass was very naturally wounded by the degradation of their superiors. Indignity to George Rose would be felt by the smallest nummary gentleman in the king's employ; and Mr. John Bannister could not be indifferent to anything which happened to Mr. Canning. But the truth is, it is a most egregious mistake to suppose that the Catholics are contending merely for the fringes and feathers of their chiefs. I will give you a list in my next Letter of those privations which are represented to be of no consequence to anybody but Lord Fingal, and some twenty or thirty of the principal persons of their sect. In the meantime, adieu, and be wise.

LETTER IX.

Dear Abraham,—No Catholic can be chief Governor or Governor of this kingdom, Chancellor or Keeper of the Great Seal, Lord High Treasurer, Chief of any of the Courts of Justice, Chancellor of the Exchequer, Puisne Judge, Judge in the Admiralty, Master of the Rolls, Secretary of State, Keeper of the Privy Seal, Vice-Treasurer or his Deputy, Teller or Cashier of Exchequer, Auditor or General, Governor or Custos Rotulorum of Counties, Chief Governor's Secretary,

Privy Councillor, King's Counsel, Serjeant, Attorney, Solicitor-General, Master in Chancery, Provost or Fellow of Trinity College, Dublin, Postmaster-General, Master and Lieutenant-General of Ordnance, Commander-in-Chief, General on the Staff, Sheriff, Sub- Sheriff, Mayor, Bailiff, Recorder, Burgess, or any other officer in a City, or a Corporation. No Catholic can be guardian to a Protestant, and no priest guardian at all; no Catholic can be a gamekeeper, or have for sale, or otherwise, any arms or warlike stores; no Catholic can present to a living, unless he choose to turn Jew in order to obtain that privilege; the pecuniary qualification of Catholic jurors is made higher than that of Protestants, and no relaxation of the ancient rigorous code is permitted, unless to those who shall take an oath prescribed by 13 and 14 George III. Now if this is not picking the plums out of the pudding and leaving the mere batter to the Catholics, I know not what is. If it were merely the Privy Council, it would be (I allow) nothing but a point of honour for which the mass of Catholics were contending, the honour of being chief-mourners or pall-bearers to the country; but surely no man will contend that every barrister may not speculate upon the possibility of being a Puisne Judge; and that every shopkeeper must not feel himself injured by his exclusion from borough offices.

One of the greatest practical evils which the Catholics suffer in Ireland is their exclusion from the offices of Sheriff and Deputy Sheriff. Nobody who is unacquainted with Ireland can conceive the obstacles which this opposes to the fair administration of justice. The formation of juries is now entirely in the hands of the Protestants; the lives, liberties, and properties of the Catholics in the hands of the juries; and this is the arrangement for the administration of justice in a country where religious prejudices are inflamed to the greatest degree of animosity! In this country, if a man be a foreigner, if he sell slippers, and sealing wax, and artificial flowers, we are so tender of human life that we take care half the number of persons who are to decide upon his fate should be men of similar prejudices and feelings with himself: but a poor Catholic in Ireland may be tried by twelve Percevals, and destroyed according to the manner of that gentleman in the name of the Lord, and with all the insulting forms of justice. I do not go the length of saying that deliberate and wilful injustice is done. I have no doubt that the Orange Deputy Sheriff thinks it would be a most unpardonable breach of his duty if he did not summon a Protestant panel. I can easily believe that the Protestant panel may conduct themselves very conscientiously in hanging the gentlemen of the crucifix; but I blame the law which does not guard the Catholic against the probable tenor of those feelings which must unconsciously influence the judgments of mankind. I detest that state of society which extends unequal degrees of protection to different creeds and persuasions; and I cannot describe to you the contempt I feel for a man who, calling himself a statesman, defends a system which fills the heart of every Irishman with treason, and makes his allegiance prudence, not choice.

I request to know if the vestry taxes in Ireland are a mere matter of romantic feeling which can affect only the Earl of Fingal? In a parish where there are four thousand Catholics and fifty Protestants, the Protestants may meet together in a vestry meeting at which no Catholic has the right to vote, and tax all the lands in the parish 1s. 6d. per acre, or in the pound, I forget which, for the repairs of the church—and how has the necessity of these repairs been ascertained? A Protestant plumber has discovered that it wants new leading; a Protestant carpenter is convinced the timbers are not sound; and the glazier who hates holy water (as an accoucheur hates celibacy, because he gets nothing by it) is employed to put in new sashes.

The grand juries in Ireland are the great scene of jobbing. They have a power of making a county rate to a considerable extent for roads, bridges, and other objects of general accommodation. "You suffer the road to be brought through my park, and I will have the bridge constructed in a situation where it will make a beautiful object to your house. You do my job, and I will do yours." These are the sweet and interesting subjects which occasionally occupy Milesian gentlemen while they are attendant upon this grand inquest of justice. But there is a religion, it seems, even in jobs; and it will be highly gratifying to Mr. Perceval to learn that no man in Ireland who believes in seven sacraments can carry a public road, or bridge, one yard out of the direction most beneficial to the public, and that nobody can cheat the public who does not expound the Scriptures in the purest and most orthodox manner. This will give pleasure to Mr. Perceval: but, from his unfairness upon these topics I appeal to the justice and the proper feelings of Mr. Huskisson. I ask him if the human mind can experience a more dreadful sensation than to see its own jobs refused, and the jobs of another religion perpetually succeeding? I ask him his opinion of a jobless faith, of a creed which dooms a man through life to a lean and plunderless integrity. He knows that human nature cannot and will not bear it; and if we were to paint a political Tartarus, it would be an endless series of snug expectations and cruel disappointments. These are a few of many dreadful inconveniences which the Catholics of all ranks suffer from the laws by which they are at present oppressed. Besides, look at human nature: what is the history of all professions? Joel is to be brought up to the bar: has Mrs. Plymley the slightest doubt of his being Chancellor? Do not his two shrivelled aunts live in the certainty of seeing him in that situation, and of cutting out with their own hands his equity habiliments? And I could name a certain minister of the Gospel who does not, in the bottom of his heart, much differ from these opinions. Do you think that the fathers and mothers of the holy Catholic Church are not as absurd as Protestant papas and mammas? The probability I admit to be, in each particular case, that the sweet little blockhead will in fact never get a brief;—but I will venture to say, there is not a parent from the Giant's Causeway to Bantry Bay who does not conceive that his child is the unfortunate victim of the exclusion, and that nothing short of positive law could prevent his own dear, pre-eminent Paddy from rising to the highest honours of the State. So with the army and parliament; in fact, few are excluded; but, in imagination, all: you keep twenty or thirty Catholics out, and you lose the affections of four millions; and, let me tell you, that recent circumstances have by no means tended to diminish in the minds of men that hope of elevation beyond their own rank which is so congenial to our nature: from pleading for John Roe to taxing John Bull, from jesting for Mr. Pitt and writing in the Anti-Jacobin, to managing the affairs of Europe—these are leaps which seem to justify the fondest dreams of mothers and of aunts.

I do not say that the disabilities to which the Catholics are exposed amount to such intolerable grievances, that the strength and industry of a nation are overwhelmed by them: the increasing prosperity of Ireland fully demonstrates to the contrary. But I repeat again, what I have often stated in the course of our correspondence, that your laws against the

Catholics are exactly in that state in which you have neither the benefits of rigour nor of liberality: every law which prevented the Catholic from gaining strength and wealth is repealed; every law which can irritate remains; if you were determined to insult the Catholics, you should have kept them weak; if you resolved to give them strength, you should have ceased to insult them—at present your conduct is pure, unadulterated folly.

Lord Hawkesbury says, "We heard nothing about the Catholics till we began to mitigate the laws against them; when we relieved them in part from this oppression they began to be disaffected. This is very true; but it proves just what I have said, that you have either done too much or too little; and as there lives not, I hope, upon earth, so depraved a courtier that he would load the Catholics with their ancient chains, what absurdity it is, then, not to render their dispositions friendly, when you leave their arms and legs free!

You know, and many Englishmen know, what passes in China; but nobody knows or cares what passes in Ireland. At the beginning of the present reign no Catholic could realise property, or carry on any business; they were absolutely annihilated, had had no more agency in the country than so many trees. They were like Lord Mulgrave's eloquence and Lord Camden's wit; the legislative bodies did not know of their existence. For these twenty-five years last past the

Catholics have been engaged in commerce; within that period the commerce of Ireland has doubled—there are four Catholics at work for one Protestant, and eight Catholics at work for one Episcopalian. Of course, the proportion which Catholic wealth bears to Protestant wealth is every year altering rapidly in favour of the Catholics. I have already told you what their purchases of land were the last year: since that period I have been at some pains to find out the actual state of the Catholic wealth: it is impossible upon such a subject to arrive at complete accuracy; but I have good reason to believe that there are at present 2,000 Catholics in Ireland, possessing an income of 500 pounds and upwards, many of these with incomes of one, two, three, and four thousand, and some amounting to fifteen and twenty thousand per annum:- and this is the kingdom, and these the people, for whose conciliation we are to wait Heaven knows when, and Lord Hawkesbury why! As for me, I never think of the situation of Ireland without feeling the same necessity for immediate interference as I should do if I saw blood flowing from a great artery. I rush towards it with the instinctive rapidity of a man desirous of preventing death, and have no other feeling but that in a few seconds the patient may be no more.

I could not help smiling, in the times of No Popery, to witness the loyal indignation of many persons at the attempt made by the last ministry to do something for the relief of Ireland. The general cry in the country was, that they would not see their beloved Monarch used ill in his old age, and that they would stand by him to the last drop of their blood. I respect good feelings, however erroneous be the occasions on which they display themselves; and therefore I saw in all this as much to admire as to blame. It was a species of affection, however, which reminded me very forcibly of the attachment displayed by the servants of the Russian ambassador at the beginning of the last century. His Excellency happened to fall down in a kind of apoplectic fit, when he was paying a morning visit in the house of an acquaintance. The confusion was of course very great, and messengers were despatched in every direction to find a surgeon: who, upon his arrival, declared that his Excellency must be immediately blooded, and prepared himself forthwith to perform the operation: the barbarous servants of the embassy, who were there in great numbers, no sooner saw the surgeon prepared to wound the arm of their master with a sharp, shining instrument, than they drew their swords, put themselves in an attitude of defence, and swore in pure Sclavonic, "that they would murder any man who attempted to do him the slightest injury: he had been a very good master to them, and they would not desert him in his misfortunes, or suffer his blood to be shed while he was off his guard, and incapable of defending himself." By good fortune, the secretary arrived about this period of the dispute, and his Excellency, relieved from superfluous blood and perilous affection, was, after much difficulty, restored to life.

There is an argument brought forward with some appearance of plausibility in the House of Commons, which certainly merits an answer: You know that the Catholics now vote for members of parliament in Ireland, and that they outnumber the Protestants in a very great proportion; if you allow Catholics to sit in parliament, religion will be found to influence votes more than property, and the greater part of the 100 Irish members who are returned to parliament will be Catholics. Add to these the Catholic members who are returned in England, and you will have a phalanx of heretical strength which every minister will be compelled to respect, and occasionally to conciliate by concessions incompatible with the interests of the Protestant Church. The fact is, however, that you are at this moment subjected to every danger of this kind which you can possibly apprehend hereafter. If the spiritual interests of the voters are more powerful than their temporal interests, they can bind down their representatives to support any measures favourable to the Catholic religion, and they can change the objects of their choice till they have found Protestant members (as they easily may do) perfectly obedient to their wishes. If the superior possessions of the Protestants prevent the Catholics from uniting for a common political object, then the danger you fear cannot exist: if zeal, on the contrary, gets the better of acres, then the danger at present exists, from the right of voting already given to the Catholics, and it will not be increased by allowing them to sit in parliament. There are, as nearly as I can recollect, thirty seats in Ireland for cities and counties, where the Protestants are the most numerous, and where the members returned must of course be Protestants. In the other seventy representations the wealth of the Protestants is opposed to the number of the Catholics; and if all the seventy members returned were of the Catholic persuasion, they must still plot the destruction of our religion in the midst of 588 Protestants. Such terrors would disgrace a cook-maid, or a toothless aunt—when they fall from the lips of bearded and senatorial men, they are nauseous, antiperistaltic, and emetical.

How can you for a moment doubt of the rapid effects which would be produced by the emancipation? In the first place, to my certain knowledge the Catholics have long since expressed to his Majesty's Ministers their perfect readiness TO VEST IN HIS MAJESTY, EITHER WITH THE CONSENT OF THE POPE, OR WITHOUT IT IF IT CANNOT BE OBTAINED, THE NOMINATION OF THE CATHOLIC PRELACY. The Catholic prelacy in Ireland consists of twenty-six bishops and the warden of Galway, a dignitary enjoying Catholic jurisdiction. The number of Roman Catholic priests in Ireland exceeds one thousand. The expenses of his peculiar worship are, to a substantial farmer or mechanic, five shillings per annum; to a labourer (where he is not entirely excused) one shilling per annum; this includes the contribution of the whole family, and for this the priest is bound to attend them when sick, and to confess them when they apply to him; he is also to keep his chapel in order, to celebrate divine service, and to preach on Sundays and holydays.

In the northern district a priest gains from 30 to 50 pounds; in the other parts of Ireland from 60 to 90 pounds per annum. The best paid Catholic bishops receive about 400 pounds per annum; the others from 300 to 350 pounds. My plan is very simple: I would have 300 Catholic parishes at 100 pounds per annum, 300 at 200 pounds per annum, and 400 at 300 pounds per annum; this, for the whole thousand parishes, would amount to 190,000 pounds. To the prelacy I would allot 20,000 pounds in unequal proportions, from 1,000 to 500 pounds; and I would appropriate 40,000 pounds more for the support of Catholic schools, and the repairs of Catholic churches; the whole amount of which sum is 250,000 pounds, about the expense of three days of one of our genuine, good English JUST AND NECESSARY WARS. The clergy should all receive their salaries at the Bank of Ireland, and I would place the whole patronage in the hands of the Crown. Now, I appeal to any human being, except Spencer Perceval, Esq., of the parish of Hampstead, what the disaffection of a clergy would amount to, gaping after this graduated bounty of the Crown, and whether Ignatius Loyala himself, if he were a living blockhead instead of a dead saint, could withstand the temptation of bouncing from 100 pounds a year at Sligo, to 300 pounds in Tipperary? This is the miserable sum of money for which the merchants and landowners and nobility of England are exposing themselves to the tremendous peril of losing Ireland. The sinecure places of the Roses and the Percevals, and the "dear and near relations," put up to auction at thirty years' purchase, would almost amount to the money.

I admit that nothing can be more reasonable than to expect that a Catholic priest should starve to death, genteelly and pleasantly, for the good of the Protestant religion; but is it equally reasonable to expect that he should do so for the Protestant pews, and Protestant brick and mortar? On an Irish Sabbath, the bell of a neat parish church often summons to church only the parson and an occasionally conforming clerk; while, two hundred yards off, a thousand Catholics are huddled together in a miserable hovel, and pelted by all the storms of heaven. Can anything be more distressing than to see a venerable man pouring forth sublime truths in tattered breeches, and depending for his food upon the little offal he gets from his parishioners? I venerate a human being who starves for his principles, let them be what they may; but starving for anything is not at all to the taste of the honourable flagellants: strict principles, and good pay, is the motto of Mr. Perceval: the one he keeps in great measure for the faults of his enemies, the other for himself.

There are parishes in Connaught in which a Protestant was never settled nor even seen. In that province in Munster, and in parts of Leinster, the entire peasantry for sixty miles are Catholics; in these tracts the churches are frequently shut for want of a congregation, or opened to an assemblage of from six to twenty persons. Of what Protestants there are in Ireland, the greatest part are gathered together in Ulster, or they live in towns. In the country of the other three provinces the Catholics see no other religion but their own, and are at the least as fifteen to one Protestant. In the diocese of Tuam they are sixty to one; in the parish of St. Mulins, diocese of Leghlin, there are four thousand Catholics and one Protestant; in the town of Grasgenamana, in the county of Kilkenny, there are between four and five hundred Catholic houses, and three Protestant houses. In the parish of Allen, county Kildare, there is no Protestant, though it is very populous. In the parish of Arlesin, Queen's County, the proportion is one hundred to one. In the whole county of Kilkenny, by actual enumeration, it is seventeen to one; in the diocese of Kilmacduagh, province of Connaught, fifty-two to one, by ditto. These I give you as a few specimens of the present state of Ireland; and yet there are men impudent and ignorant enough to contend that such evils require no remedy, and that mild family man who dwelleth in Hampstead can find none but the cautery and the knife.

- "Omne per ignem
Excoquitur vitium."

I cannot describe the horror and disgust which I felt at hearing Mr. Perceval call upon the then Ministry for measures of vigour in Ireland. If I lived at Hampstead upon stewed meats and claret; if I walked to church every Sunday before eleven young gentlemen of my own begetting, with their faces washed, and their hair pleasingly combed; if the Almighty had blessed me with every earthly comfort— how awfully would I pause before I sent forth the flame and the sword over the cabins of the poor, brave, generous, open-hearted peasants of Ireland! How easy it is to shed human blood; how easy it is to persuade ourselves that it is our duty to do so, and that the decision has cost us a severe struggle; how much in all ages have wounds and shrieks and tears been the cheap and vulgar resources of the rulers of mankind; how difficult and how noble it is to govern in kindness and to found an empire upon the everlasting basis of justice and affection! But what do men call vigour? To let loose hussars and to bring up artillery, to govern with lighted matches, and to cut, and push, and prime; I call this not vigour, but the SLOTH OF CRUELTY AND IGNORANCE. The vigour I love consists in finding out wherein subjects are aggrieved, in relieving them, in studying the temper and genius of a people, in consulting their prejudices, in selecting proper persons to lead and manage them, in the laborious, watchful, and difficult task of increasing public happiness by allaying each particular discontent. In this way Hoche pacified La Vendee—and in this way only will Ireland ever be subdued. But this, in the eyes of Mr. Perceval, is imbecility and meanness. Houses are not broken open, women are not insulted, the people seem all to be happy; they are not rode over by horses, and cut by whips. Do you call this vigour? Is this government?

LETTER X. AND LAST.

You must observe that all I have said of the effects which will be produced by giving salaries to the Catholic clergy, only proceeds upon the supposition that the emanciptaion of the laity is effected: —without that, I am sure there is not a clergyman in Ireland who would receive a shilling from government; he could not do so, without an entire loss of credit among the members of his own persuasion.

What you say of the moderation of the Irish Protestant clergy in collecting tithes, is, I believe, strictly true. Instead of collecting what the law enables them to collect, I believe they seldom or ever collect more than two-thirds; and I entirely agree with you, that the abolition of agistment tithe in Ireland by a vote of the Irish House of Commons, and without any remuneration to the Church, was a most scandalous and Jacobinical measure. I do not blame the Irish clergy; but I submit to your common sense, if it be possible to explain to an Irish peasant upon what principle of justice, or common sense, he is to pay every tenth potato in his little garden to a clergyman in whose religion nobody believes for twenty miles around him, and who has nothing to preach to but bare walls? It is true, if the tithes are bought up, the cottager must pay more rent to his landlord; but the same thing done in the shape of rent is less odious than when it is done in the shape of tithe. I do not want to take a shilling out of the pockets of the clergy, but to leave the substance of things, and to change their names. I cannot see the slightest reason why the Irish labourer is to be relieved from the real onus, or from anything else but the name of tithe. At present he rents only nine-tenths of the produce of the land, which is all that belongs to the owner; this he has at the market price; if the landowner purchase the other tenth of the Church, of course he has a right to make a correspondent advance upon his tenant.

I very much doubt, if you were to lay open all civil offices to the Catholics, and to grant salaries to their clergy, in the manner I have stated, if the Catholic laity would give themselves much trouble about the advance of their Church; for they would pay the same tithes under one system that they do under another. If you were to bring the Catholics into the daylight of the world, to the high situations of the army, the navy, and the bar, numbers of them would come over to the Established Church, and do as other people do; instead of that, you set a mark of infamy upon them, rouse every passion of our nature in favour of their creed, and then wonder that men are blind to the follies of the Catholic religion. There are hardly any instances of old and rich families among the Protestant Dissenters: when a man keeps a coach, and lives in good company, he comes to church, and gets ashamed of the meeting-house; if this is not the case with the father, it is almost always the case with the son. These things would never be so if the Dissenters were in PRACTICE as much excluded from all the concerns of civil life as the Catholics are. If a rich young Catholic were in Parliament, he would belong to White's and to Brookes's, would keep race-horses, would walk up and down Pall Mall, be exonerated of his ready money and his constitution, become as totally devoid of morality, honesty, knowledge, and civility as Protestant loungers in Pall Mall, and return home with a supreme contempt for Father O'Leary and Father O'Callaghan. I am astonished at the madness of the Catholic clergy in not perceiving that Catholic emancipation is Catholic infidelity; that to entangle their people in the intrigues of a Protestant parliament, and a Protestant court, is to ensure the loss of every man of fashion and consequence in their community. The true receipt for preserving their religion, is Mr. Perceval's receipt for destroying it: it is to deprive every rich Catholic of all the objects of secular ambition, to separate him from the Protestant, and to shut him up in his castle with priests and relics.

We are told, in answer to all our arguments, that this is not a fit period—that a period of universal war is not the proper time for dangerous innovations in the constitution: this is as much as to say, that the worst time for making friends is the period when you have made many enemies; that it is the greatest of all errors to stop when you are breathless, and to lie down when you are fatigued. Of one thing I am quite certain: if the safety of Europe is once completely restored, the Catholics may for ever bid adieu to the slightest probability of effecting their object. Such men as hang about a court not only are deaf to the suggestions of mere justice, but they despise justice; they detest the word RIGHT; the only word which rouses them is PERIL; where they can oppress with impunity, they oppress for ever, and call it loyalty and wisdom.

I am so far from conceiving the legitimate strength of the Crown would be diminished by these abolitions of civil incapacities in consequence of religious opinions, that my only objection to the increase of religious freedom is, that it would operate as a diminution of political freedom; the power of the Crown is so overbearing at this period, that almost the only steady opposers of its fatal influence are men disgusted by religious intolerance. Our establishments are so enormous, and so utterly disproportioned to our population, that every second or third man you meet in society gains something from the public; my brother the commissioner,—my nephew the police justice,—purveyor of small beer to the army in Ireland,—clerk of the mouth,— yeoman to the left hand,—these are the obstacles which common sense and justice have now to overcome. Add to this that the King, old and infirm, excites a principle of very amiable generosity in his favour; that he has led a good, moral, and religious life, equally removed from profligacy and methodistical hypocrisy; that he has been a good husband, a good father, and a good master; that he dresses plain, loves hunting and farming, fates the French, and is in all his opinions and habits, quite English: —these feelings are heightened by the present situation of the world, and the yet unexploded clamour of Jacobinism. In short, from the various sources of interest, personal regard, and national taste, such a tempest of loyalty has set in upon the people that the 47th proposition in Euclid might now be voted down with as much ease as any proposition in politics; and therefore if Lord Hawkesbury hates the abstract truths of science as much as he hates concrete truth in human affairs, now is his time for getting rid of the multiplication table, and passing a vote of censure upon the pretensions of the hypotenuse. Such is the history of English parties at this moment: you cannot seriously suppose that the people care for such men as Lord Hawkesbury, Mr. Canning, and Mr. Perceval on their own account; you cannot really believe them to be so degraded as to look to their safety from a man who proposes to subdue Europe by keeping it without Jesuit's Bark. The people at present have one passion, and but one -

"A Jove principium, Jovis omnia plena."

They care no more for the ministers I have mentioned, than they do for those sturdy royalists who for 60 pounds per annum stand behind his Majesty's carriage, arrayed in scarlet and in gold. If the present ministers opposed the Court instead of flattering it, they would not command twenty votes.

Do not imagine by these observations that I am not loyal; without joining in the common cant of the best of kings, I respect the King most sincerely as a good man. His religion is better than the religion of Mr. Perceval, his old morality very superior to the old morality of Mr. Canning, and I am quite certain he has a safer understanding than both of them put together. Loyalty within the bounds of reason and moderation is one of the great instruments of human happiness; but the love of the king may easily become more strong than the love of the kingdom, and we may lose sight of the public welfare in our exaggerated admiration of him who is appointed to reign only for its promotion and support. I detest Jacobinism; and if I am doomed to be a slave at all, I would rather be the slave of a king than a cobbler. God save the King, you say, warms your heart like the sound of a trumpet. I cannot make use of so violent a metaphor; but I am delighted to hear it, when it is the cry of genuine affection; I am delighted to hear it when they hail not only the individual man, but the outward and living sign of all English blessings. These are noble feelings, and the heart of every good man must go with them; but God save the King, in these times, too often means God save my pension and my place, God give my sisters an allowance out of the privy purse—make me clerk of the irons, let me survey the meltings, let me live upon the fruits of other men's industry, and fatten upon the plunder of the public.

What is it possible to say to such a man as the Gentleman of Hampstead, who really believes it feasible to convert the four million Irish Catholics to the Protestant religion, and considers this as the best remedy for the disturbed state of Ireland? It is not possible to answer such a man with arguments; we must come out against him with beads and a cowl, and push him into an hermitage. It is really such trash, that it is an abuse of the privilege of reasoning to reply to it. Such a project is well worthy the statesman who would bring the French to reason by keeping them without rhubarb, and exhibit to mankind the awful spectacle of a nation deprived of neutral salts. This is not the dream of a wild apothecary indulging in his own opium; this is not the distempered fancy of a pounder of drugs, delirious from smallness of profits; but it is the sober, deliberate, and systematic scheme of a man to whom the public safety is intrusted, and whose appointment is considered by many as a masterpiece of political sagacity. What a sublime thought, that no purge can now be taken between the Weser and the Garonne; that the bustling pestle is still, the canorous mortar mute, and the bowels of mankind locked up for fourteen degrees of latitude! When, I should be curious to know, were all the powers of crudity and flatulence fully explained to his Majesty's ministers? At what period was this great plan of conquest and constipation fully developed? In whose mind was the idea of destroying the pride and the plasters of France first engendered? Without castor oil they might for some months, to be sure, have carried on a lingering war! but can they do without bark? Will the people live under a government where antimonial powders cannot be procured? Will they bear the loss of mercury? "There's the rub." Depend upon it, the absence of the materia medica will soon bring them to their senses, and the cry of Bourbon and bolus burst forth from the Baltic to the Mediterranean.

You ask me for any precedent in our history where the oath of supremacy has been dispensed with. It was dispensed with to the Catholics of Canada in 1774. They are only required to take a simple oath of allegiance. The same, I believe, was the case in Corsica. The reason of such exemption was obvious; you could not possibly have retained either of these countries without it. And what did it signify, whether you retained them or not? In cases where you might have been foolish without peril you were wise; when nonsense and bigotry threaten you with destruction, it is impossible to bring you back to the alphabet of justice and common sense. If men are to be fools, I would rather they were fools in little matters than in great; dulness turned up with temerity is a livery all the worse for the facings; and the most tremendous of all things is the magnanimity of the dunce.

It is not by any means necessary, as you contend, to repeal the Test Act if you give relief to the Catholic: what the Catholics ask for is to be put on a footing with the Protestant Dissenters, which would be done by repealing that part of the law which compels them to take the oath of supremacy and to make the declaration against transubstantiation: they would then come into Parliament as all other Dissenters are allowed to do, and the penal laws to which they were exposed for taking office would be suspended every year, as they have been for this half century past towards Protestant Dissenters.

Perhaps, after all, this is the best method—to continue the persecuting law, and to suspend it every year—a method which, while it effectually destroys the persecution itself, leaves to the great mass of mankind the exquisite gratification of supposing that they are enjoying some advantage from which a particular class of their fellow creatures are excluded. We manage the Corporation and Test Acts at present much in the same manner as if we were to persuade parish boys who had been in the habit of beating an ass to spare the animal, and beat the skin of an ass stuffed with straw; this would preserve the semblance of tormenting without the reality, and keep boy and beast in good humour.

How can you imagine that a provision for the Catholic clergy affects the 5th article of the Union? Surely I am preserving the Protestant Church in Ireland if I put it in a better condition than that in which it now is. A tithe proctor in Ireland collects his tithes with a blunderbuss, and carries his tenth hay-cock by storm, sword in hand: to give him equal value in a more pacific shape cannot, I should imagine, be considered as injurious to the Church of Ireland; and what right has that Church to complain if Parliament chooses to fix upon the empire the burden of supporting a double ecclesiastical establishment? Are the revenues of the Irish Protestant clergy in the slightest degree injured by such provision? On the contrary, is it possible to confer a more serious benefit upon that Church than by quieting and contenting those who are at work for its destruction?

It is impossible to think of the affairs of Ireland without being forcibly struck with the parallel of Hungary. Of her seven millions of inhabitants, one half were Protestants, Calvinists, and Lutherans, many of the Greek Church, and many Jews: such was the state of their religious dissensions that Mahomet had often been called in to the aid of Calvin, and the crescent often glittered on the walls of Buda and Presburg. At last, in 1791, during the most violent crisis of disturbance, a Diet was called, and by a great majority of voices a decree was passed, which secured to all the contending sects the fullest and freest exercise of religious worship and education; ordained—let it be heard in Hampstead—that churches and chapels should be erected for all on the most perfectly equal terms; that the Protestants of both confessions should depend upon their spiritual superiors alone; liberated them from swearing by the usual oath, "the Holy Virgin Mary, the saints, and chosen of God;" and then the decree adds, "that PUBLIC OFFICES AND HONOURS, HIGH OR LOW, GREAT OR SMALL, SHALL BE GIVEN TO NATURAL-BORN HUNGARIANS WHO DESERVE WELL OF THEIR COUNTRY, AND POSSESS THE OTHER QUALIFICATIONS, LET THEIR RELIGION BE WHAT IT MAY." Such was the line of policy pursued in a Diet consisting of four hundred members, in a state whose form of government approaches nearer to our own than any other, having a Roman Catholic establishment of great wealth and power, and under the influence of one of the most bigoted Catholic Courts in Europe. This measure has now the experience of eighteen years in its favour; it has undergone a trial of fourteen years of revolution such as the world never witnessed, and more than equal to a century less convulsed: What have been its effects? When the French advanced like a torrent within a few days' march of Vienna, the Hungarians rose in a mass; they formed what they called the sacred insurrection, to defend their sovereign, their rights and liberties, now common to all; and the apprehension of their approach dictated to the reluctant Bonaparte the immediate signature of the treaty of Leoben. The Romish hierarchy of Hungary exists in all its former splendour and opulence; never has the slightest attempt been made to diminish it; and those revolutionary principles, to which so large a portion of civilised Europe has been sacrificed, have here failed in making the smallest successful inroad.

The whole history of this proceeding of the Hungarian Diet is so extraordinary, and such an admirable comment upon the Protestantism of Mr. Spencer Perceval, that I must compel you to read a few short extracts from the law itself: —"The Protestants of both confessions shall, in religious matters, depend upon their own spiritual superiors alone. The Protestants may likewise retain their trivial and grammar schools. The Church dues which the Protestants have hitherto paid to the Catholic parish priests, schoolmasters, or other such officers, either in money, productions, or labour, shall in future entirely cease, and after three months from the publishing of this law, be no more anywhere demanded. In the building or repairing of churches, parsonage-houses, and schools, the Protestants are not obliged to assist the Catholics with labour, nor the Catholics the Protestants. The pious foundations and donations of the Protestants which already exist, or which in future may be made for their churches, ministers, schools and students, hospitals, orphan houses, and poor, cannot be taken from them under any pretext, nor yet the care of them; but rather the unimpeded administration shall be intrusted to those from among them to whom it legally belongs, and those foundations which may have been taken from them under the last government shall be returned to them without delay. All affairs of marriage of the Protestants are left to their own consistories; all landlords and masters of families, under the penalty of public prosecution, are ordered not to prevent their subjects and servants, whether they be Catholic or Protestant, from the observance of the festivals and ceremonies of their religion," etc. etc. etc.—By what strange chances are mankind influenced! A little Catholic barrister of Vienna might have raised the cry of NO PROTESTANTISM, and Hungary would have panted for the arrival of a French army as much as Ireland does at this moment; arms would have been searched for; Lutheran and Calvinist houses entered in the dead of the night; and the strength of Austria exhausted in guarding a country from which, under the present liberal system, she may expect in the moment of danger the most powerful aid: and let it be remembered that this memorable example of political wisdom took place at a period when many great monarchies were yet unconquered in Europe; in a country where the two religious parties were equal in number; and where it is impossible to suppose indifference in the party which relinquished its exclusive privileges. Under all these circumstances the measure was carried in the Hungarian Diet by a majority of 280 to 120. In a few weeks we shall see every concession denied to the Catholics by a much larger majority of Protestants, at a moment when every other power is subjugated but ourselves, and in a country where the oppressed are four times as numerous as their oppressors. So much for the wisdom of our ancestors—so much for the nineteenth century- -so much for the superiority of the English over all the nations of the Continent.

Are you not sensible, let me ask you, of the absurdity of trusting the lowest Catholics with offices correspondent to their situation in life, and of denying such privileges to the higher. A Catholic may serve in the militia, but a Catholic cannot come into Parliament; in the latter case you suspect combination, and in the former case you suspect no combination; you deliberately arm ten or twenty thousand of the lowest of the Catholic people; and the moment you come to a class of men whose education, honour, and talents seem to render all mischief less probable, then you see the danger of employing a Catholic, and cling to your investigating tests and disabling laws. If you tell me you have enough of members of Parliament and not enough of militia without the Catholics, I beg leave to remind you that, by employing the physical force of any sect at the same time when you leave them in a state of utter disaffection, you are not adding strength to your armies, but weakness and ruin. If you want the vigour of their common people, you must not disgrace their nobility and insult their priesthood.

I thought that the terror of the Pope had been confined to the limits of the nursery, and merely employed as a means to induce young master to enter into his small-clothes with greater speed and to eat his breakfast with greater attention to decorum. For these purposes the name of the Pope is admirable; but why push it beyond? Why not leave to Lord Hawkesbury all further enumeration of the Pope's powers? For a whole century you have been exposed to the enmity of France, and your succession was disputed in two rebellions: what could the Pope do at the period when there was a serious struggle whether England should be Protestant or Catholic, and when the issue was completely doubtful? Could the Pope induce the Irish to rise in 1715? Could he induce them to rise in 1745? You had no Catholic enemy when half this island was in arms; and what did the Pope attempt in the last rebellion in Ireland? But if he had as much power over the minds of the Irish as Mr. Wilberforce has over the mind of a young Methodist converted the preceding quarter, is this a reason why we are to disgust men who may be acted upon in such a manner by a foreign power? or is it not an additional reason why we should raise up every barrier of affection and kindness against the mischief of foreign influence? But the true answer is, the mischief does not exist. Gog and Magog have produced as much influence upon human affairs as the Pope has done for this half century past; and by spoiling him of his possessions, and degrading him in the eyes of all Europe, Bonaparte has not taken quite the proper method of increasing his influence.

But why not a Catholic king as well as a Catholic member of Parliament, or of the Cabinet?—Because it is probable that the one would be mischievous and the other not. A Catholic king might struggle against the Protestantism of the country, and if the struggle were not successful it would at least be dangerous; but the efforts of any other Catholic would be quite insignificant, and his hope of success so small, that it is quite improbable the effort would ever be made: my argument is, that in so Protestant a country as Great Britain, the character of her parliaments and her cabinet could not be changed by the few Catholics who would ever find their way to the one or the other. But the power of the Crown is immeasurably greater than the power which the Catholics could obtain from any other species of authority in the state; and it does not follow because the lesser degree of power is innocent that the greater should be so too. As for the stress you lay upon the danger of a Catholic chancellor, I have not the least hesitation in saying that his appointment would not do a ten thousandth part of the mischief to the English Church that might be done by a Methodistical chancellor of the true Clapham breed; and I request to know if it is really so very necessary that a chancellor should be of the religion of the Church of England, how many chancellors you have had within the last century who have been bred up in the Presbyterian religion? And again, how many you have had who notoriously have been without any religion at all?

Why are you to suppose that eligibility and election are the same thing, and that all the cabinet WILL be Catholics whenever all the cabinet MAY be Catholics? You have a right, you say, to suppose an extreme case, and to argue upon it—so have I: and I will suppose that the hundred Irish members will one day come down in a body and pass a law compelling the King to reside in Dublin. I will suppose that the Scotch members, by a similar stratagem, will lay England under a large contribution of meal and sulphur: no measure is without objection if you sweep the whole horizon for danger; it is not sufficient to tell me of what may happen, but you must show me a rational probability that it will happen: after all, I might, contrary to my real opinion, admit all your dangers to exist; it is enough for me to contend that all other dangers taken together are not equal to the danger of losing Ireland from disaffection and invasion.

I am astonished to see you, and many good and well-meaning clergymen beside you, painting the Catholics in such detestable colours; two- thirds, at least, of Europe are Catholics—they are Christians, though mistaken Christians; how can I possibly admit that any sect of Christians, and, above all, that the oldest and the most numerous sect of Christians are incapable of fulfilling the common duties and relations of life: though I do differ from them in many particulars, God forbid I should give such a handle to infidelity, and subscribe to such blasphemy against our common religion?

Do you think mankind never change their opinions without formally expressing and confessing that change? When you quote the decisions of ancient Catholic councils, are you prepared to defend all the decrees of English convocations and universities since the reign of Queen Elizabeth? I could soon make you sick of your uncandid industry against the Catholics, and bring you to allow that it is better to forget times past, and to judge and be judged by present opinions and present practice.

I must beg to be excused from explaining and refuting all the mistakes about the Catholics made by my Lord Redesdale; and I must do that nobleman the justice to say, that he has been treated with great disrespect. Could anything be more indecent than to make it a morning lounge in Dublin to call upon his Lordship, and to cram him with Arabian-night stories about the Catholics? Is this proper behaviour to the representative of Majesty, the child of Themis, and the keeper of the conscience in West Britain? Whoever reads the Letters of the Catholic Bishops, in the appendix to Sir John Hippesly's very sensible book, will see to what an excess this practice must have been carried with the pleasing and Protestant nobleman whose name I have mentioned, and from thence I wish you to receive your answer about excommunication, and all the trash which is talked against the Catholics.

A sort of notion has, by some means or another, crept into the world that difference of religion would render men unfit to perform together the offices of common and civil life: that Brother Wood and Brother Grose could not travel together the same circuit if they differed in creed, nor Cockell and Mingay be engaged in the same cause, if Cockell was a Catholic and Mingay a Muggletonian. It is supposed that Huskisson and Sir Harry Englefield would squabble behind the Speaker's chair about the council of Lateran, and many a turnpike bill miscarry by the sarcastical controversies of

Mr. Hawkins Brown and Sir John Throckmorton upon the real presence. I wish I could see some of these symptoms of earnestness upon the subject of religion; but it really seems to me that, in the present state of society, men no more think about inquiring concerning each other's faith than they do concerning the colour of each other's skins. There may have been times in England when the quarter sessions would have been disturbed by theological polemics; but now, after a Catholic justice had once been seen on the bench, and it had been clearly ascertained that he spoke English, had no tail, only a single row of teeth, and that he loved port wine—after all the scandalous and infamous reports of his physical conformation had been clearly proved to be false— he would be reckoned a jolly fellow, and very superior in flavour to a sly Presbyterian. Nothing, in fact, can be more uncandid and unphilosophical than to say that a man has a tail, because you cannot agree within him upon religious subjects; it appears to be ludicrous: but I am convinced it has done infinite mischief to the Catholics, and made a very serious impression upon the minds of many gentlemen of large landed property.

In talking of the impossibility of Catholic and Protestant living together with equal privilege under the same government, do you forget the Cantons of Switzerland? You might have seen there a Protestant congregation going into a church which had just been quitted by a Catholic congregation; and I will venture to say that the Swiss Catholics were more bigoted to their religion than any people in the whole world. Did the kings of Prussia ever refuse to employ a Catholic? Would Frederick the Great have rejected an able man on this account? We have seen Prince Czartorinski, a Catholic Secretary of State in Russia; in former times a Greek patriarch and an apostolic vicar acted together in the most perfect harmony in Venice; and we have seen the Emperor of Germany in modern times intrusting the care of his person and the command of his guard to a Protestant Prince, Frederick of Wittenberg. But what are all these things to Mr. Perceval? He has looked at human nature from the top of Hampstead Hill, and has not a thought beyond the little sphere of his own vision. "The snail," say the Hindoos, "sees nothing but his own shell, and thinks it the grandest palace in the universe."

I now take a final leave of this subject of Ireland; the only difficulty in discussing it is a want of resistance, a want of something difficult to unravel, and something dark to illumine. To agitate such a question is to beat the air with a club, and cut down gnats with a scimitar; it is a prostitution of industry, and a waste of strength. If a man say, I have a good place, and I do not choose to lose it, this mode of arguing upon the Catholic question I can well understand; but that any human being with an understanding two degrees elevated above that of an Anabaptist preacher, should conscientiously contend for the expediency and propriety of leaving the Irish Catholics in their present state, and of subjecting us to such tremendous peril in the present condition of the world, it is utterly out of my power to conceive. Such a measure as the Catholic question is entirely beyond the common game of politics; it is a measure in which all parties ought to acquiesce, in order to preserve the place where and the stake for which they play. If Ireland is gone, where are jobs? where are reversions? where is my brother Lord Arden? where are my dear and near relations? The game is up, and the Speaker of the house of Commons will be sent as a present to the menagerie at Paris. We talk of waiting from particular considerations, as if centuries of joy and prosperity were before us: in the next ten years our fate must be decided; we shall know, long before that period, whether we can bear up against the miseries by which we are threatened or not; and yet, in the very midst of our crisis, we are enjoined to abstain from the most certain means of increasing our strength, and advised to wait for the remedy till the disease is removed by death or health. And now, instead of the plain and manly policy of increasing unanimity at home, by equalising rights and privileges, what is the ignorant, arrogant, and wicked system which has been pursued? Such a career of madness and of folly was, I believe, never run in so short a period. The vigour of the ministry is like the vigour of a grave-digger—the tomb becomes more ready and more wide for every effort which they make. There is nothing which it is worth while either to take or to retain, and a constant train of ruinous expeditions have been kept up. Every Englishman felt proud of the integrity of his country; the character of the country is lost for ever. It is of the utmost consequence to a commercial people at war with the greatest part of Europe, that there should be a free entry of neutrals into the enemy's ports; the neutrals who earned our manufactures we have not only excluded, but we have compelled them to declare war against us. It was our interest to make a good peace, or convince our own people that it could not be obtained; we have not made a peace, and we have convinced the people of nothing but of the arrogance of the Foreign Secretary: and all this has taken place in the short space of a year, because a King's Bench barrister and a writer of epigrams, turned into Ministers of State, were determined to show country gentlemen that the late administration had no vigour. In the meantime commerce stands still, manufactures perish, Ireland is more and more irritated, India is threatened, fresh taxes are accumulated upon the wretched people, the war is carried on without it being possible to conceive any one single object which a rational being can propose to himself by its continuation; and in the midst of this unparalleled insanity we are told that the Continent is to be reconquered by the want of rhubarb and plums. A better spirit than exists in the English people never existed in any people in the world: it has been misdirected, and squandered upon party purposes in the most degrading and scandalous manner; they have been led to believe that they were benefiting the commerce of England by destroying the commerce of America, that they were defending their Sovereign by perpetuating the bigoted oppression of their fellow-subjects; their rulers and their guides have told them that they would equal the vigour of France by equalling her atrocity; and they have gone on wasting that opulence, patience, and courage, which, if husbanded by prudent and moderate counsels, might have proved the salvation of mankind. The same policy of turning the good qualities of Englishmen to their own destruction, which made Mr. Pitt omnipotent, continues his power to those who resemble him only in his vices; advantage is taken of the loyalty of Englishmen to make them meanly submissive; their piety is turned into persecution, their courage into useless and obstinate contention; they are plundered because they are ready to pay, and soothed into asinine stupidity because they are full of virtuous patience. If England must perish at last, so let it be: that event is in the hands of God; we must dry up our tears and submit. But that England should perish swindling and stealing; that it should perish waging war against lazar houses and hospitals; that it should perish persecuting with monastic bigotry; that it should calmly give itself up to be ruined by the flashy arrogance of one man, and the narrow fanaticism of another;

these events are within the power of human beings, and I did not think that the magnanimity of Englishmen would ever stoop to such degradations.

Longum Vale!
PETER PLYMLEY.

HISTORICAL APOLOGY FOR THE IRISH CATHOLICS.

Historical Apology for The Irish Catholics. By WILLIAM PARNELL, Esquire. Fitzpatrick, Dublin. 1807.

If ever a nation exhibited symptoms of downright madness, or utter stupidity, we conceive these symptoms may be easily recognised in the conduct of this country upon the Catholic question. A man has a wound in his great toe, and a violent and perilous fever at the same time; and he refuses to take the medicines for the fever because it will disconcert the toe! The mournful and folly-stricken blockhead forgets that his toe cannot survive him; that if he dies, there can be no digital life apart from him: yet he lingers and fondles over this last part of his body, soothing it madly with little plasters, and anile fomentations, while the neglected fever rages in his entrails, and burns away his whole life. If the comparatively little questions of Establishment are all that this country is capable of discussing or regarding, for God's sake let us remember that the foreign conquest, which destroys all, destroys this beloved TOE also. Pass over freedom, industry, and science—and look upon this great empire, by which we are about to be swallowed up, only as it affects the manner of collecting tithes, and of reading the liturgy—still, if all goes, these must go too; and even, for their interests, it is worth while to conciliate Ireland, to avert the hostility, and to employ the strength of the Catholic population. We plead the question as the sincerest friends to the Establishment;— as wishing to it all the prosperity and duration its warmest advocates can desire,—but remembering always what these advocates seem to forget, that the Establishment cannot be threatened by any danger so great as the perdition of the kingdom in which it is established.

We are truly glad to agree so entirely with Mr. Parnell upon this great question; we admire his way of thinking, and most cordially recommend his work to the attention of the public. The general conclusion which he attempts to prove is this: that religious sentiment, however perverted by bigotry or fanaticism, has always a TENDENCY to moderation.; that it seldom assumes any great portion of activity or enthusiasm, except from novelty of opinion, or from opposition, contumely, and persecution, when novelty ceases; that a Government has little to fear from any religious sect, except while that sect is new. Give a Government only time, and, provided it has the good sense to treat folly with forbearance, it must ultimately prevail. When, therefore, a sect is found, after a lapse of years, to be ill-disposed to the Government, we may be certain that Government has widened its separation by marked distinctions, roused its resentment by contumely, or supported its enthusiasm by persecution.

The PARTICULAR conclusion Mr. Parnell attempts to prove is, that the Catholic religion in Ireland had sunk into torpor and inactivity, till Government roused it with the lash: that even then, from the respect and attachment which men are always inclined to show towards government, there still remained a large body of loyal Catholics; that these only decreased in number from the rapid increase of persecution; and that, after all, the effects which the resentment of the Roman Catholics had in creating rebellions had been very much exaggerated.

In support of these two conclusions, Mr. Parnell takes a survey of the history of Ireland, from the conquest under Henry to the rebellion under Charles I., passing very rapidly over the period which preceded the Reformation, and dwelling principally upon the various rebellions which broke out in Ireland between the Reformation and the grand rebellion in the reign of Charles I. The celebrated conquest of Ireland by Henry II. extended only to a very few counties in Leinster; nine-tenths of the whole kingdom were left, as he found them, under the dominion of their native princes. The influence of example was as strong in this as in most other instances; and great numbers of the English settlers who came over under various adventures resigned their pretensions to superior civilisation, cast off their lower garments, and lapsed into the nudity and barbarism of the Irish. The limit which divided the possessions of the English settler from those of the native Irish was called THE PALE; and the expressions of inhabitants WITHIN THE PALE, and WITHOUT THE PALE, were the terms by which the two nations were distinguished. It is almost superfluous to state, that the most bloody and pernicious warfare was carried on upon the borders— sometimes for something, sometimes for nothing—most commonly for cows. The Irish, over whom the sovereigns of England affected a sort of nominal dominion, were entirely governed by their own laws, and so very little connection had they with the justice of the invading country, that it was as lawful to kill an Irishman as it was to kill a badger or a fox. The instances are innumerable, where the defendant has pleaded that the deceased was an Irishman, and that therefore defendant had a right to kill him—and upon the proof of Hibernicism, acquittal followed of course.

When the English army mustered in any great strength, the Irish chieftains would do exterior homage to the English Crown; and they very frequently, by this artifice, averted from their country the miseries of invasion: but they remained completely unsubdued, till the rebellion which took place in the reign of Queen Elizabeth, of which that politic woman availed herself to the complete subjugation of Ireland. In speaking of the Irish about the reign of Elizabeth or James I., we must not draw our comparisons from England, but from New Zealand; they were not civilised men, but savages; and if we reason about their conduct, we must reason of them as savages.

"After reading every account of Irish history," says Mr. Parnell, "one great perplexity appears to remain: How does it happen, that, from the first invasion of the English till the reign of James I., Ireland seems not to have made the smallest progress in civilisation or wealth?

"That it was divided into a number of small principalities, which waged constant war on each other—or that the appointment of the chieftains was elective—do not appear sufficient reasons, although these are the only ones assigned by those who have been at the trouble of considering the subject: neither are the confiscations of property quite sufficient to account for the effect. There have been great confiscations in other countries, and still they have flourished; the petty states of Greece were quite analogous to the chiefries, as they were called, in Ireland; and yet they seemed to flourish almost in proportion to their dissensions. Poland felt the bad effects of an elective monarchy more than any other country; and yet, in point of civilisation, it maintained a very respectable rank among the nations of Europe; but Ireland never, for an instant, made any progress in improvement, till the reign of James I.

"It is scarcely credible, that in a climate like that of Ireland, and at a period so far advanced in civilisation as the end of Elizabeth's reign, the greater part of the natives should go naked. Yet this is rendered certain by the testimony of an eye-witness, Fynes Moryson. 'In the remote parts,' he says, 'where the English laws and manners are unknown, the very chief of the Irish, as well men as women, go naked in the winter time, only having their privy parts covered with a rag of linen, and their bodies with a loose mantle. This I speak of my own experience; yet remember that a Bohemian baron coming out of Scotland to us by the north parts of the wild Irish, told me in great earnestness, that he, coming to the house of O'Kane, a great lord amongst them, was met at the door by sixteen women, all naked, excepting their loose mantles, whereof eight or ten were very fair; with which strange sight his eyes being dazzled, they led him into the house, and then sitting down by the fire, with crossed legs, like tailors, and so low as could not but offend chaste eyes, desired him to sit down with them. Soon after, O'Kane, the lord of the country, came in all naked, except a loose mantle and shoes, which he put off as soon as he came in; and, entertaining the Baron after his best manner in the Latin tongue, desired him to put off his apparel, which he thought to be a burden to him, and to sit naked.

"'To conclude, men and women at night going to sleep, he thus naked in a round circle about the fire, with their feet towards it. They fold their heads and their upper parts in woollen mantles, first steeped in water to keep them warm; for they say, that woollen cloth, wetted, preserves heat (as linen, wetted, preserves cold), when the smoke of their bodies has warmed the woollen cloth.'

"The cause of this extreme poverty, and of its long continuance, we must conclude, arose from the peculiar laws of property which were in force under the Irish dynasties. These laws have been described by most writers as similar to the Kentish custom of gavelkind; and, indeed, so little attention was paid to the subject, that were it not for the researches of Sir J. Davis, the knowledge of this singular usage would have been entirely lost.

"The Brehon law of property, he tells us, was similar to the custom (as the English lawyers term it) of hodge-podge. When any one of the sept died, his lands did not descend to his sons, but were divided among the whole sept: and, for this purpose, the chief of the sept made a new division of the whole lands belonging to the sept, and gave every one his part according to seniority. So that no man had a property which could descend to his children; and even during his own life his possession of any particular spot was quite uncertain, being liable to be constantly shuffled and changed by new partitions. The consequence of this was that there was not a house of brick or stone among the Irish down to the reign of Henry VII.; not even a garden or orchard, or well-fenced or improved field; neither village or town, or in any respect the least provision for posterity. This monstrous custom, so opposite to the natural feelings of mankind, was probably perpetuated by the policy of the chiefs. In the first place the power of partitioning being lodged in their hands, made them the most absolute of tyrants, being the dispensers of the property as well as of the liberty of their subjects. In the second place, it had the appearance of adding to the number of their savage armies; for where there was no improvement or tillage, war was pursued as an occupation.

"In the early history of Ireland, we find several instances of chieftains discountenancing tillage; and so late as Elizabeth's reign, Moryson says, that 'Sir Neal Garve restrained his people from ploughing, that they might assist him to do any mischief.'"

These quotations and observations will enable us to state a few plain facts for the recollection of our English readers: —lst, Ireland was never subdued till the rebellion in the reign of Queen Elizabeth. 2nd, For four hundred years before that period the two nations had been almost constantly at war; and in consequence of this, a deep and irreconcilable hatred existed between the people within and without the pale. 3rd, The Irish, at the accession of Queen Elizabeth, were unquestionably the most barbarous people in Europe. So much for what had happened previous to the reign of Queen Elizabeth; and let any man, who has the most superficial knowledge of human affairs, determine whether national hatred, proceeding from such powerful causes, could possibly have been kept under by the defeat of one single rebellion—whether it would not have been easy to have foreseen, at that period, that a proud, brave, half-savage people, would cherish the memory of their wrongs for centuries to come, and break forth into arms at every period when they were particularly exasperated by oppression, or invited by opportunity. If the Protestant religion had spread in Ireland as it did in England, and if there had never been any difference of faith between the two countries—can it be believed that the Irish, ill- treated and infamously governed as they have been, would never have made any efforts to shake off the yoke of England? Surely there are causes enough to account for their impatience of that yoke, without endeavouring to inflame the zeal of ignorant people against the Catholic religion, and to make that mode of faith responsible for all the butchery which the Irish and English for these last two centuries have exercised upon each other. Everybody, of course, must admit, that if to the causes of hatred already specified there be added the additional cause of religious distinction, this last will give greater force (and what is of more consequence to observe, give a NAME) to the whole aggregate motive. But what Mr. Parnell contends for, and clearly and decisively proves, is that many of those sanguinary scenes attributed to the Catholic religion are to be partly imputed to causes totally disconnected from religion; that the unjust invasion, and the tyrannical, infamous policy of the English, are to take their full share of blame with the sophisms and plots of Catholic priests. In the reign of Henry VIII., Mr. Parnell shows that feudal submission was readily paid to him by all the Irish chiefs; that the Reformation was received without the slightest opposition; and that the troubles which took place at that period in Ireland are to be entirely attributed to the ambition and injustice of Henry. In the reign of Queen Mary there was no recrimination upon the Protestants—a striking proof that the bigotry of the Catholic religion had not at that period risen to any great height in Ireland. The insurrections of the various Irish princes were as numerous during this reign as they had been in the two preceding reigns—a circumstance rather difficult of explanation, if, as is commonly believed, the Catholic religion was at that period the main-spring of men's actions.

In the reign of Elizabeth, the Catholic in the pale regularly fought against the Catholic out of the pale. O'Sullivan, a bigoted Papist, reproaches them with doing so. Speaking of the reign of James I., he says, "And now the eyes even of the English Irish (the Catholics of the pale) were opened; and they cursed their former folly for helping the heretic." The English Government were so sensible of the loyalty of the Irish English Catholics that they entrusted them with the most confidential services. The Earl of Kildare was the principal instrument in waging war against the chieftains of Leix and Offal. William O'Bourge, another

Catholic, was created Lord Castle Connel for his eminent services; and MacGully Patrick, a priest, was the State spy. We presume that this wise and MANLY conduct of Queen Elizabeth was utterly unknown both to the Pastrycook and the Secretary of State, who have published upon the dangers of employing Catholics even against foreign enemies; and in those publications have said a great deal about the wisdom of our ancestors—the usual topic whenever the folly of their descendants is to be defended. To whatever other of our ancestors they may allude, they may spare all compliments to this illustrious Princess, who would certainly have kept the worthy confectioner to the composition of tarts, and most probably furnished him with the productions of the Right Honourable Secretary as the means of conveying those juicy delicacies to a hungry and discerning public.

In the next two reigns, Mr. Parnell shows by what injudicious measures of the English Government the spirit of Catholic opposition was gradually formed; for that it did produce powerful effects at a subsequent period he does not deny; but contends only (as we have before stated) that these effects have been much overrated, and ascribed SOLELY to the Catholic religion when other causes have at least had an equal agency in bringing them about. He concludes with some general remarks on the dreadful state of Ireland, and the contemptible folly and bigotry of the English—remarks full of truth, of good sense, and of political courage. How melancholy to reflect, that there would be still some chance of saving England from the general wreck of empires, but that it may not be saved, because one politician will lose two thousand a year by it, and another three thousand—a third a place in reversion, and a fourth a pension for his aunt! Alas! these are the powerful causes which have always settled the destiny of great kingdoms, and which may level Old England, with all its boasted freedom, and boasted wisdom, to the dust. Nor is it the least singular, among the political phenomena of the present day, that the sole consideration which seems to influence the unbigoted part of the English people, in this great question of Ireland, is a regard for the personal feelings of the Monarch. Nothing is said or thought of the enormous risk to which Ireland is exposed—nothing of the gross injustice with which the Catholics are treated— nothing of the lucrative apostasy of those from whom they experience this treatment: but the only concern by which we all seem to be agitated is, that the King must not be vexed in his old age. We have a great respect for the King; and wish him all the happiness compatible with the happiness of his people. But these are not times to pay foolish compliments to kings, or the sons of kings, or to anybody else; this journal (the Edinburgh Review) has always preserved its character for courage and honesty; and it shall do so to the last. If the people of this country are solely occupied in considering what is personally agreeable to the King, without considering what is for his permanent good, and for the safety of his dominions; if all public men, quitting the common vulgar scramble for emolument, do not concur in conciliating the people of Ireland; if the unfounded alarms, and the comparatively trifling interests of the clergy, are to supersede the great question of freedom or slavery, it does appear to us quite impossible that so mean and so foolish a people can escape that destruction which is ready to burst upon them—a destruction so imminent that it can only be averted by arming all in our defence who would evidently be sharers in our ruin—and by such a change of system as may save us from the hazard of being ruined by the ignorance and cowardice of any general, by the bigotry or the ambition of any minister, or by the well-meaning scruples of any human being, let his dignity be what it may. These minor and domestic dangers we must endeavour firmly and temperately to avert as we best can; but at all hazards we must keep out the destroyer from among us, or perish like wise and brave men in the attempt.

IRELAND AND ENGLAND

1. Whitelaw's History of the City of Dublin. 4to. Cadell and Davies.

2. Observations on the State of Ireland, principally directed to its Agriculture and Rural Population; in a Series of Letters written on a Tour through that Country. In 2 vols. By J. C. Curwen, Esq., M.P. London, 1818.

3. Gamble's Views of Society in Ireland.

These are all the late publications that treat of Irish interests in general, and none of them are of first-rate importance. Mr. Gamble's "Travels in Ireland" are of a very ordinary description, low scenes and low humour making up the principal part of the narrative. There are readers, however, whom it will amuse; and the reading market becomes more and more extensive, and embraces a greater variety of persons every day. Mr. Whitelaw's "History of Dublin" is a book of great accuracy and research, highly creditable to the industry, good sense, and benevolence of its author. Of the "Travels" of Mr. Christian Curwen we hardly know what to say. He is bold and honest in his politics, a great enemy to abuses, vapid in his levity and pleasantry, and infinitely too much inclined to declaim upon commonplace topics of morality and benevolence. But, with these drawbacks, the book is not ill-written, and may be advantageously read by those who are desirous of information upon the present state of Ireland.

So great and so long has been the misgovernment of that country, that we verily believe the empire would be much stronger if everything was open sea between England and the Atlantic, and if SKATES AND COD-FISH swam over the fair land of Ulster. Such jobbing, such profligacy, so much direct tyranny and oppression, such an abuse of God's gifts, such a profanation of God's name for the purposes of bigotry and party spirit, cannot be exceeded in the history of civilised Europe, and will long remain a monument of infamy and shame to England. But it will be more useful to suppress the indignation which the very name of Ireland inspires, and to consider impartially those causes which have marred this fair portion of the creation, and kept it wild and savage in the midst of improving Europe.

The great misfortune of Ireland is that the mass of the people have been given up for a century to a handful of Protestants, by whom they have been treated as Helots, and subjected to every species of persecution and disgrace. The sufferings of the Catholics have been so loudly chanted in the very streets, that it is almost needless to remind our readers that, during the reigns of George I. and George

II., the Irish Roman Catholics were disabled from holding any civil or military office, from voting at elections, from admission into corporations, from practising law or physic. A younger brother, by turning Protestant, might deprive his elder brother of his birthright; by the same process he might force his father, under the name of a liberal provision, to yield up to him a part of his landed property; and, if an eldest son, he might, in the same way, reduce his father's fee-simple to a life-estate. A Papist was disabled from purchasing freehold lands, and even from holding long leases; and any person might take his Catholic neighbour's house by paying 5 pounds for it. If the child of a Catholic father turned Protestant he was taken away from his father and put into the hands of a Protestant relation. No Papist could purchase a freehold or lease for more than thirty years, or inherit from an intestate Protestant, nor from an intestate Catholic, nor dwell in Limerick or Galway, nor hold an advowson, nor buy an annuity for life. 50 pounds was given for discovering a Popish archbishop, 30 pounds for a Popish clergyman, and 10s. for a schoolmaster. No one was allowed to be trustee for Catholics; no Catholic was allowed to take more than two apprentices; no Papist to be solicitor, sheriff, or to serve on Grand Juries. Horses of Papists might be seized for the militia, for which militia Papists were to pay double, and to find Protestant substitutes. Papists were prohibited from being present at vestries, or from being high or petty constables:

and, when resident in towns, they were compelled to find Protestant watchmen. Barristers and solicitors marrying Catholics were exposed to the penalties of Catholics. Persons plundered by privateers during a war with any Popish prince were reimbursed by a levy on the Catholic inhabitants where they lived. All Popish priests celebrating marriages contrary to 12 Geo. I., cap 3, were to be HANGED!

The greater part of these incapacities are removed, though many of a very serious and oppressive nature still remain. But the grand misfortune is that the spirit which these oppressive laws engendered remains. The Protestant still looks upon the Catholic as a degraded being. The Catholic does not yet consider himself upon an equality with his former tyrant and taskmaster. That religious hatred which required all the prohibiting vigilance of the law for its restraint has found in the law its strongest support; and the spirit which the law first exasperated and embittered continues to act long after the original stimulus is withdrawn. The law which prevented Catholics from serving on Grand Juries is repealed; but Catholics are not called upon Grand Juries in the proportion in which they are entitled by their rank and fortune. The Duke of Bedford did all he could to give them the benefit of those laws which are already passed in their favour. But power is seldom entrusted in this country to one of the Duke of Bedford's liberality, and everything has fallen back in the hands of his successors into the ancient division of the privileged and degraded castes. We do not mean to cast any reflection upon the present Secretary for Ireland, whom we believe to be upon this subject a very liberal politician, and on all subjects an honourable and excellent man. The Government under which he serves allows him to indulge in a little harmless liberality; but it is perfectly understood that nothing is intended to be done for the Catholics; that no loaves and fishes will be lost by indulgence in Protestant insolence and tyranny; and, therefore, among the generality of Irish Protestants, insolence, tyranny, and exclusion continue to operate. However eligible the Catholic may be, he is not elected; whatever barriers may be thrown down, he does not advance a step. He was first kept out by law; he is now kept out by opinion and habit. They have been so long in chains that nobody believes they are capable of using their hands and feet.

It is not, however, the only or the worst misfortune of the Catholics that the relaxations of the law are hitherto of little benefit to them; the law is not yet sufficiently relaxed. A Catholic, as everybody knows, cannot be made sheriff; cannot be in parliament; cannot be a director of the Irish Bank; cannot fill the great departments of the law, the army, and the navy; is cut off from all the high objects of human ambition, and treated as a marked and degraded person.

The common admission now is that the Catholics are to the Protestants in Ireland as about four to one, of which Protestants not more than ONE HALF belong to the Church of Ireland. This, then, is one of the most striking features in the state of Ireland. That the great mass of the population is completely subjugated and overawed by a handful of comparatively recent settlers, in whom all the power and patronage of the country is vested, who have been reluctantly compelled to desist from still greater abuses of authority, and who look with trembling apprehension to the increasing liberality of the parliament and the country towards these unfortunate persons whom they have always looked upon as their property and their prey.

Whatever evils may result from these proportions between the oppressor and oppressed—to whatever dangers a country so situated may be considered to be exposed, these evils and dangers are rapidly increasing in Ireland. The proportion of Catholics to Protestants is infinitely greater now than it was thirty years ago, and is becoming more and more favourable to the former. By a return made to the Irish House of Lords in 1732 the proportion of Catholics to Protestants was not two to one. It is now (as we have already observed) four to one; and the causes which have thus altered the proportions in favour of the Catholics are sufficiently obvious to any one acquainted with the state of Ireland. The Roman Catholic priest resides; his income entirely depends upon the number of his flock; and he must exert himself or he starves. There is some chance of success, therefore, in

HIS efforts to convert; but the Protestant clergyman, if he were equally eager, has little or no probability of persuading so much larger a proportion of the population to come over to his Church. The Catholic clergyman belongs to a religion that has always been more desirous of gaining proselytes than the Protestant Church; and he is animated by a sense of injury and a desire of revenge. Another reason for the disproportionate increase of Catholics is that the Catholics will marry upon means which the Protestant considers as insufficient for marriage. A few potatoes and a shed of turf are all that Luther has left for the Romanist; and, when the latter gets these, he instantly begins upon the great Irish manufacture of children. But a Protestant belongs to the sect that eats the fine flour and heaves the bran to others; he must have comforts, and he does not marry till he gets them. He would be ashamed if he were seen living as a Catholic lives. This is the principal reason why the Protestants who remain attached to their Church do not increase so fast as the Catholics. But in common minds, daily scenes, the example of the majority, the power of imitation, decide their habits, religious as well as civil. A Protestant labourer who works among Catholics soon learns to think and act and talk as they do; he is not proof against the eternal panegyric which he hears of Father O'Leary. His Protestantism is rubbed away, and he goes at last, after some little resistance, to the chapel where he sees everybody else going.

These eight Catholics not only hate the ninth man, the Protestant of the Establishment, for the unjust privileges he enjoys—not only remember that the lands of their father were given to his father— but they find themselves forced to pay for the support of his religion. In the wretched state of poverty in which the lower orders of Irish are plunged, it is not without considerable effort that they can pay the few shillings necessary for the support of their Catholic priest; and when this is effected, a tenth of the potatoes in the garden are to be set out for the support of a persuasion, the introduction of which into Ireland they consider as the great cause of their political inferiority, and all their manifold wretchedness. In England a labourer can procure constant employment, or he can, at the worst, obtain relief from his parish. Whether tithe operates as a tax upon him, is known only to the political economist: if he does pay it, he does not know that he pays it, and the burden of supporting the Clergy is at least kept out of his view. But in Ireland, the only method in which a poor man lives is by taking a small portion of land in which he can grow potatoes: seven or eight months out of twelve, in many parts of Ireland, there is no constant employment of the poor; and the potato farm is all that shelters them from absolute famine. If the Pope were to come in person, seize upon every tenth potato, the poor peasant would scarcely endure it. With what patience, then, can he see it tossed into the cart of the heretic rector, who has a church without a congregation, and a revenue without duties? We do not say whether these things are right or wrong, whether they want a remedy at all, or what remedy they want; but we paint them in those colours in which they appear to the eye of poverty and ignorance, without saying whether those colours are false or true. Nor is the case at all comparable to that of Dissenters paying tithe in England; which case is precisely the reverse of what happens in Ireland, for it is the contribution of a very small minority to the religion of a very large majority; and the numbers on either side make all the difference in the argument. To exasperate the poor Catholic still more, the rich graziers of the parish, or the squire in his parish, pay no tithe at all for their grass land. Agistment tithe is abolished in Ireland, and the burthen of supporting two Churches seems to devolve upon the poorer Catholics, struggling with plough and spade in small scraps of dearly-rented land. Tithes seem to be collected in a more harsh manner than they are collected in England. The minute sub-divisions of land in Ireland—the little connection which the Protestant clergyman commonly has with the Catholic population of his parish—have made the introduction of tithe proctors very general, sometimes as the agent of the clergyman, sometimes as the lessee or middleman between the clergyman and the cultivator of the land, but, in either case, practised, dexterous estimators of tithe. The English clergymen in general are far from exacting the whole of what is due to them, but sacrifice a little to the love of popularity or to the dread of odium. A system of tithe- proctors established all over England (as it is in Ireland), would produce general disgust and alienation from the Established Church.

"During the administration of Lord Halifax," says Mr. Hardy, in quoting the opinion of Lord Charlemont upon tithes paid by Catholics, "Ireland was dangerously disturbed in its southern and northern regions. In the south principally, in the counties of Kilkenny, Limerick, Cork, and Tipperary, the White Boys now made their first appearance; those White Boys who have ever since occasionally disturbed the public tranquillity, without any rational method having been as yet pursued to eradicate this disgraceful evil. When we consider that the very same district has been for the long space of seven-and-twenty years liable to frequent returns of the same disorder into which it has continually relapsed, in spite of all the violent remedies from time to time administered by our political quacks, we cannot doubt but that some real, peculiar, and topical cause must exist, and yet neither the removal, nor even the investigation of this cause, has ever once been seriously attempted. Laws of the most sanguinary and unconstitutional nature have been enacted; the country has been disgraced and exasperated by frequent and bloody executions; and the gibbet, that perpetual resource of weak and cruel legislators, has groaned under the multitude of starving criminals; yet, while the cause is suffered to exist, the effects will ever follow. The amputation of limbs will never eradicate a prurient humour, which must be sought in its source and there remedied."

"I wish," continues Mr. Wakefield, "for the sake of humanity and for the honour of the Irish character, that the gentlemen of that country would take this matter into their serious consideration. Let them only for a moment place themselves in the situation of the half-famished cotter, surrounded by a wretched family clamorous for food, and judge what his feelings must be when he sees the tenth part of the produce of his potato garden exposed at harvest time to public CANT, or if he have given a promissory note for the payment of a certain sum of money to compensate for such tithe when it becomes due, to hear the heart-rending cries of his offspring clinging round him, and lamenting for the milk of which they are deprived by the cows being driven to the pound to be sold to discharge the debt. Such accounts are not the creations of fancy; the facts do exist, and are but too common in Ireland. Were one of them transferred to canvas by the hand of genius, and exhibited to English humanity, that heart must be callous indeed that could refuse its sympathy. I have seen the cow, the favourite cow, driven away, accompanied by the sighs, the tears, and the imprecations of a whole family, who were paddling after, through wet and dirt, to take their last affectionate farewell of this their only friend and benefactor at the pound gate. I have heard with emotions which I can scarcely describe, deep curses repeated from village to village as the cavalcade proceeded. I have witnessed the group pass the domain walls of the opulent grazier, whose numerous herds were cropping the most luxuriant pastures, while he was secure from any demand for the tithe of their food, looking on with the most unfeeling indifference."—Ibid., p. 486.

In Munster, where tithe of potatoes is exacted, risings against the system have constantly occurred during the last forty years. In Ulster, where no such tithe is required, these insurrections are unknown. The double Church which Ireland supports, and that painful visible contribution towards it which the poor Irishman is compelled to make from his miserable pittance, is one great cause of those never-ending insurrections, burnings, murders, and robberies, which have laid waste that ill-fated country for so many years. The unfortunate consequence of the civil disabilities, and the Church payments under which the Catholics labour, is a rooted antipathy to this country. They hate the English Government from historical recollection, actual suffering, and disappointed hope, and till they are better treated they will continue to hate it. At this moment, in a period of the most profound peace, there are twenty-five thousand of the best disciplined and best appointed troops in the world in Ireland, with bayonets fixed, presented arms, and in the attitude of present war: nor is there a man too much—nor would Ireland be tenable without them. When it was necessary last year (or thought necessary) to put down the children of reform, we were forced to make a new levy of troops in this country; not a man could be spared from Ireland. The moment they had embarked, Peep-of-Day Boys, Heart-of-Oak Boys, Twelve-o'-clock Boys, Heart-of-Flint Boys, and all the bloody boyhood of the Bog of Allen, would have proceeded to the ancient work of riot, rapine, and disaffection. Ireland, in short, till her wrongs are redressed and a more liberal policy is adopted towards her, will always be a cause of anxiety and suspicion to this country, and in some moment of our weakness and depression, will forcibly extort what she would now receive with gratitude and exultation.

Ireland is situated close to another island of greater size, speaking the same language, very superior in civilisation, and the seat of government. The consequence of this is the emigration of the richest and most powerful part of the community—a vast drain of wealth—and the absence of all that wholesome influence which the representatives of ancient families, residing upon their estates, produce upon their tenantry and dependents. Can any man imagine that the scenes which have been acted in Ireland, within these last twenty years, would have taken place, if such vast proprietors as the Duke of Devonshire, the Marquis of Hertford, the

Marquis of Lansdowne, Earl Fitzwilliam, and many other men of equal wealth, had been in the constant habit of residing upon their Irish as they are upon their English estates? Is it of no consequence to the order and the civilisation of a large district, whether the great mansion is inhabited by an insignificant, perhaps a mischievous attorney, in the shape of agent, or whether the first and greatest men of the United Kingdoms, after the business of Parliament is over, come with their friends and families, to exercise hospitality, to spend large revenues, to diffuse information, and to improve manners? This evil is a very serious one to Ireland; and, as far as we see, incurable. For if the present large estates were, by the dilapidation of families, to be broken to pieces and sold, others equally great would, in the free circulation of property, speedily accumulate; and the moment any possessor arrived at a certain pitch of fortune, he would probably choose to reside in the better country—near the Parliament, or the Court.

This absence of great proprietors in Ireland necessarily brings with it, or if not necessarily, has actually brought with it, the employment of the middlemen, which forms one other standing and regular Irish grievance. We are well aware of all that can be said in defence of middlemen; that they stand between the little farmer and the great proprietor as the shopkeeper does between the manufacturer and consumer; and, in fact, by their intervention, save time, and therefore expense. This may be true enough in the abstract; but the particular nature of land must be attended to. The object of the man who makes cloth is to sell his cloth at the present market, for as high a price as he can obtain. If that price is too high, it soon falls; but no injury is done to his machinery by the superior price he has enjoyed for a season—he is just as able to produce cloth with it, as if the profits he enjoyed had always been equally moderate; he has no fear, therefore, of the middleman, or of any species of moral machinery which may help to obtain for him the greatest present prices. The same would be the feeling of any one who let out a steam-engine, or any other machine, for the purposes of manufacture; he would naturally take the highest price he could get; for he might either let his machine for a price proportionate to the work it did, or the repairs, estimable with the greatest precision, might be thrown upon the tenant; in short, he could hardly ask any rent too high for his machine which a responsible person would give; dilapidation would be so visible, and so calculable in such instances, that any secondary lease, or subletting, would be rather an increase of security than a source of alarm. Any evil from such a practice would be improbable measurable, and remediable. In land, on the contrary, the object is not to get the highest prices absolutely, but to get the highest prices which will not injure the machine. One tenant may offer and pay double the rent of another, and in a few years leave the land in a state which will effectually bar all future offers of tenancy. It is of no use to fill a lease full of clauses and covenants; a tenant who pays more than he ought to pay, or who pays even to the last farthing which he ought to pay, will rob the land, and injure the machine, in spite of all the attorneys in England. He will rob it even if he means to remain upon it—driven on by present distress, and anxious to put off the day of defalcation and arrear. The damage is often difficult of detection—not easily calculated, not easily to be proved; such for which juries (themselves perhaps farmers) will not willingly give sufficient compensation. And if this be true in England, it is much more strikingly true in Ireland, where it is extremely difficult to obtain verdicts for breaches of covenant in leases.

The only method, then, of guarding the machine from real injury, is by giving to the actual occupier such advantage in his contract, that he is unwilling to give it up—that he has a real interest in retaining it, and is not driven by the distresses of the present moment to destroy the future productiveness of the soil. Any rent which the landlord accepts more than this, or any system by which more rent than this is obtained, is to borrow money upon the most usurious and profligate interest—to increase the revenue of the present day by the absolute ruin of the property. Such is the effect produced by a middleman; he gives high prices that he may obtain higher from the occupier; more is paid by the actual occupier than is consistent with the safety and preservation of the machine; the land is run out, and, in the end, that maximum of rent we have described is not obtained; and not only is the property injured by such a system, but in Ireland the most shocking consequences ensue from it. There is little manufacture in Ireland; the price of labour is low, the demand for labour irregular. If a poor man be driven, by distress of rent, from his potato garden, he has no other resource—all is lost: he will do the impossible (as the French say) to retain it; subscribe any bond, and promise any rent. The middleman has no character to lose; and he knew, when he took up the occupation, that it was one with which pity had nothing to do. On he drives; and backward the poor peasant recedes, loses something at every step, till he comes to the very brink of despair; and then he recoils and murders his oppressor, and is a White Boy or a Right Boy;—the soldier shoots him, and the judge hangs him.

In the debate which took place in the Irish House of Commons, upon the Bill for preventing tumultuous risings and assemblies, on the 31st of January, 1787, the Attorney-General submitted to the House the following narrative of facts.

"The commencement," said he, "was in one or two parishes in the county of Kerry; and they proceeded thus. The people assembled in a Catholic chapel, and there took an oath to obey the laws of Captain Right, and to starve the clergy. They then proceeded to the next parishes on the following Sunday, and there swore the people in the same manner; with this addition, that they (the people last sworn) should on the ensuing Sunday proceed to the chapels of their next neighbouring parishes and swear the inhabitants of those parishes in like manner. Proceeding in this manner, they very soon went through the province of Munster. The first object was the REFORMATION OF TITHES. They swore not to give more than a certain price per acre, not to assist or allow them to be assisted in drawing the tithe, and to permit NO PROCTOR. They next took upon them to prevent the collection of parish cesses, next to nominate parish clerks, and in some cases curates, to say what church should or should not be repaired, and in one case to threaten that they would burn a NEW church if the OLD one were not given for a mass-house. At last they proceeded to regulate the price of lands, to raise the price of labour, and to oppose the collection of the hearth-money and other taxes. Bodies of 5,000 of them have been seen to march through the country unarmed, and, if met by any magistrate, THEY NEVER OFFERED THE SMALLEST RUDENESS OR OFFENCE; on the contrary, they had allowed persons charged with crimes to be taken from amongst them by the magistrate ALONE, unaided by any force.

"The Attorney-General said he was well acquainted with the province of Munster, and that it was impossible for human wretchedness to EXCEED THAT OF THE PEASANTRY OF THAT PROVINCE. The unhappy tenantry were GROUND TO POWDER by relentless landlords; that, far from being able to give the clergy their just dues, they had not food or raiment for themselves—the landlord grasped the whole; and sorry was he to add that, not satisfied with the present extortion, some landlords had been so base as to instigate the insurgents to rob the clergy of their tithes, not in order to alleviate the distresses of the tenantry, but that they might add the clergy's share to the cruel rack-rents they already paid. The poor people of Munster lived in a MORE ABJECT STATE OF POVERTY THAN HUMAN NATURE COULD BE SUPPOSED EQUAL TO BEAR."—"Grattan's Speeches," vol. i., p. 292.

We are not, of course, in such a discussion to be governed by names. A middleman might be tied up by the strongest legal restriction, as to the price he was to exact from the under-tenants, and then he would be no more pernicious to the estate than a steward. A steward might be protected in exactions as severe as the most rapacious middleman; and then, of course, it would be the same thing under another name. The practice to which we object is the too common method in Ireland of extorting the last farthing which the tenant is willing to give for land rather than quit it: and the machinery by which such practice is carried into effect is that of the middleman. It is not only that it ruins the land; it ruins the people also. They are made so poor—brought so near the ground—that they can sink no lower; and burst out at last into all the acts of desperation and revenge for which Ireland is so notorious. Men who have money in their pockets, and find that they are improving in their circumstances, don't do these things. Opulence, or the hope of opulence or comfort, is the parent of decency, order, and submission to the laws. A landlord in Ireland understands the luxury of carriages and horses, but has no relish for the greater luxury of surrounding himself with a moral and grateful tenantry. The absent proprietor looks only to revenue, and cares nothing for the disorder and degradation of a country which he never means to visit. There are very honourable exceptions to this charge: but there are too many living instances that it is just. The rapacity of the Irish landlord induces him to allow of the extreme division of his lands. When the daughter marries, a little portion of the little farm is broken off—another corner for Patrick, and another for Dermot—till the land is broken into sections, upon one of which an English cow could not stand. Twenty mansions of misery are thus reared instead of one. A louder cry of oppression is lifted up to heaven, and fresh enemies to the English name and power are multiplied on the earth. The Irish gentleman, too, extremely desirous of political influence, multiplying freeholds, and splitting votes; and this propensity tends of course to increase the miserable redundance of living beings, under which Ireland is groaning. Among the manifold wretchedness to which the poor Irish tenant is liable, we must not pass over the practice of driving for rent. A lets land to B, who lets it to C, who lets it again to D. D pays C his rent, and C pays B. But if B fails to pay A, the cattle of B, C, D are all driven to the pound, and after the interval of a few days sold by auction. A general driving of this kind very frequently leads to a bloody insurrection. It may be ranked among the classical grievances of Ireland.

Potatoes enter for a great deal into the present condition of Ireland. They are much cheaper than wheat; and it is so easy to rear a family upon them, that there is no cheek to population from the difficulty of procuring food. The population therefore goes on with a rapidity approaching almost to that of new countries, and in a much greater ratio than the improving agriculture and manufacturers of the country can find employment for it. All degrees of all nations begin with living in pig-styes. The king or the priest first gets out of them; then the noble, then the pauper; in proportion as each class becomes more and more opulent. Better tastes arise from better circumstances; and the luxury of one period is the wretchedness and poverty of another. English peasants, in the time of Henry VII., were lodged as badly as Irish peasants now are; but the population was limited by the difficulty of procuring a corn subsistence. The improvements of this kingdom were more rapid; the price of labour rose;

and with it the luxury and comfort of the peasant, who is now decently lodged and clothed, and who would think himself in the last stage of wretchedness if he had nothing but an iron pot in a turf house, and plenty of potatoes in it. The use of the potato was introduced into Ireland when the wretched accommodation of her own peasantry bore some proportion to the state of those accommodations all over Europe. But they have increased their population so fast, and, in conjunction with the oppressive government of Ireland retarding improvement, have kept the price of labour so low, that the Irish poor have never been able to emerge from their mud cabins, or to acquire any taste for cleanliness and decency of appearance. Mr. Curwen has the following description of Irish cottages:-

"These mansions of miserable existence, for so they may truly be described, conformably to our general estimation of those indispensable comforts requisite to constitute the happiness of rational beings, are most commonly composed of two rooms on the ground floor, a most appropriate term, for they are literally on the earth, the surface of which is not unfrequently reduced a foot or more to save the expense of so much outward walling. The one is a refectory, the other the dormitory. The furniture of the former, if the owner ranks in the upper part of the scale of scantiness, will consist of a kitchen dresser, well provided and highly decorated with crockery—not less apparently the pride of the husband than the result of female vanity in the wife: which, with a table, a chest, a few stools, and an iron pot, complete the catalogue of conveniences generally found as belonging to the cabin: while a spinning-wheel, furnished by the Linen Board, and a loom, ornament vacant spaces that otherwise would remain unfurnished. In fitting up the latter, which cannot on any occasion or by any display add a feather to the weight or importance expected to be excited by the appearance of the former, the inventory is limited to one, and sometimes two beds, serving for the repose of the whole family! However downy these may be to limbs impatient for rest, their coverings appear to be very slight, and the whole of the apartment created reflections of a very painful nature. Under such privations, with a wet mud floor and a roof in tatters, how idle the search for comforts!"—Curwen

To this extract we shall add one more on the same subject.

"The gigantic figure, bareheaded before me, had a beard that would not have disgraced an ancient Israelite—he was without shoes or stockings—and almost a sans-culotte— with a coat, or rather a jacket, that appeared as if the first blast of wind would tear it to tatters. Though his garb was thus tattered, he had a manly commanding countenance. I asked permission to see the inside of his cabin, to which I received his most courteous assent. On stooping to enter at the door I was stopped, and found that permission from another was necessary before I could be admitted. A pig, which was fastened to a stake driven into the floor, with length of rope sufficient to permit him the enjoyment of sun and air, demanded some courtesy, which I showed him, and was suffered to enter. The wife was engaged in boiling thread, and by her side, near the fire, a lovely infant was sleeping, without any covering, on a bare board. Whether the fire gave additional glow to the countenance of the babe, or that Nature impressed on its unconscious cheek a blush that the lot of man should be exposed to such privations, I will not decide; but if the cause be referable to the latter, it was in perfect unison with my own feelings. Two or three other children crowded round the mother: on their rosy countenances health seemed established in spite of filth and ragged garments. The dress of the poor woman was barely sufficient to satisfy decency. Her countenance bore the expression of a set melancholy, tinctured with an appearance of ill health. The hovel, which did not exceed twelve or fifteen feet in length and ten in breadth, was half obscured by smoke—chimney or window I saw none; the door served the various purposes of an inlet to light and the outlet to smoke. The furniture consisted of two stools, an iron pot, and a spinning- wheel, while a sack stuffed with straw, and a single blanket laid on planks, served as a bed for the repose of the whole family. Need I attempt to describe my sensations? The statement alone cannot fail of conveying to a mind like yours an adequate idea of them—I could not long remain a witness to this acme of human misery. As I left the deplorable habitation the mistress followed me to repeat her thanks for the trifle I had bestowed. This gave me an opportunity of observing her person more particularly. She was a tall figure, her countenance composed of interesting features, and with every appearance of having once been handsome.

"Unwilling to quit the village without first satisfying myself whether what I had seen was a solitary instance or a sample of its general state, or whether the extremity of poverty I had just beheld had arisen from peculiar improvidence and want of management in one wretched family, I went into an adjoining habitation, where I found a poor old woman of eighty, whose miserable existence was painfully continued by the maintenance of her granddaughter. Their condition, if possible, was more deplorable."—Curwen

This wretchedness, of which all strangers who visit Ireland are so sensible, proceeds certainly in great measure from their accidental use of a food so cheap, that it encourages population to an extraordinary degree, lowers the price of labour, and leaves the multitudes which it calls into existence almost destitute of everything but food. Many more live in consequence of the introduction of potatoes; but all live in greater wretchedness. In the progress of population, the potato must of course become at last as difficult to be procured as any other food; and then let the political economist calculate what the immensity and wretchedness of a people must be, where the further progress of population is checked by the difficulty of procuring potatoes.

The consequence of the long mismanagement and oppression of Ireland, and of the singular circumstances in which it is placed, is, that it is a semi-barbarous country— more shame to those who have thus ill- treated a fine country and a fine people; but it is part of the present case of Ireland. The barbarism of Ireland is evinced by the frequency and ferocity of duels—the hereditary clannish feuds of the common people and the fights to which they give birth— the atrocious cruelties practised in the insurrections of the common people—and their proneness to insurrection. The lower Irish live in a state of greater wretchedness than any other people in Europe inhabiting so fine a soil and climate. It is difficult, often impossible, to execute the processes of law. In cases where gentlemen are concerned, it is often not even attempted. The conduct of under-sheriffs is often very corrupt. We are afraid the magistracy of Ireland is very inferior to that of this country; the spirit of jobbing and bribery is very widely diffused, and upon occasions when the utmost purity prevails in the sister kingdom. Military force is necessary all over the country, and often for the most common and just operations of Government. The behaviour of the higher to the lower orders is much less gentle and decent than in

England. Blows from superiors to inferiors are more frequent, and the punishment for such aggression more doubtful. The word GENTLEMAN seems, in Ireland, to put an end to most processes at law. Arrest a gentleman!!!—take out a warrant against a gentleman—are modes of operation not very common in the administration of Irish justice. If a man strike the meanest peasant in England, he is either knocked down in his turn, or immediately taken before a magistrate. It is impossible to live in Ireland without perceiving the various points in which it is inferior in civilisation. Want of unity in feeling and interest among the people—irritability, violence, and revenge—want of comfort and cleanliness in the lower orders—habitual disobedience to the law— want of confidence in magistrates—corruption, venality, the perpetual necessity of recurring to military force—all carry back the observer to that remote and early condition of mankind, which an Englishman can learn only in the pages of the antiquary or the historian. We do not draw this picture for censure but for truth. We admire the Irish—feel the most sincere pity for the state of Ireland—and think the conduct of the English to that country to have been a system of atrocious cruelty and contemptible meanness. With such a climate, such a soil, and such a people, the inferiority of Ireland to the rest of Europe is directly chargeable to the long wickedness of the English Government.

A direct consequence of the present uncivilised state of Ireland is, that very little English capital travels there. The man who deals in steam-engines, and warps and woofs, is naturally alarmed by Peep- of-Day Boys, and nocturnal Carders; his object is to buy and sell as quickly and quietly as he can, and he will naturally bear high taxes and rivalry in England, or emigrate to any part of the Continent, or to America, rather than plunge into the tumult of Irish politics and passions. There is nothing which Ireland wants more than large manufacturing towns to take off its superfluous population. But internal peace must come first, and then the arts of peace will follow. The foreign manufacturer will hardly think of embarking his capital where he cannot be sure that his existence is safe. Another check to the manufacturing greatness of Ireland is the scarcity, not of coal, but of good coal, cheaply raised—an article in which (in spite of papers in the Irish Transactions) they are lamentably inferior to the English.

Another consequence from some of the causes we have stated is the extreme idleness of the Irish labourer. There is nothing of the value of which the Irish seem to have so little notion as that of time. They scratch, pick, dawdle, stare, gape, and do anything but strive and wrestle with the task before them. The most ludicrous of all human objects is an Irishman ploughing. A gigantic figure—a seven-foot machine for turning potatoes in human nature—wrapt up in an immense great-coat, and urging on two starved ponies, with dreadful imprecations and uplifted shillala. The Irish crow discerns a coming perquisite, and is not inattentive to the proceedings of the steeds. The furrow which is to be the depository of the future crop is not unlike, either in depth or regularity, to those domestic furrows which the nails of the meek and much-injured wife plough, in some family quarrel, upon the cheeks of the deservedly punished husband. The weeds seem to fall contentedly, knowing that they have fulfilled their destiny, and left behind them, for the resurrection of the ensuing spring, an abundant and healthy progeny. The whole is a scene of idleness, laziness, and poverty, of which it is impossible, in this active and enterprising country, to form the most distant conception; but strongly indicative of habits, whether secondary or original, which will long present a powerful impediment to the improvement of Ireland.

The Irish character contributes something to retard the improvements of that country. The Irishman has many good qualities: he is brave, witty, generous, eloquent, hospitable, and open-hearted; but he is vain, ostentatious, extravagant, and fond of display, light in counsel, deficient in perseverance, without skill in private or public economy, an enjoyer, not an acquirer—one who despises the slow and patient virtues—who wants the superstructure without the foundation, the result without the previous operation, the oak without the acorn and the three hundred years of expectation. The Irish are irascible, prone to debt and to fight, and very impatient of the restraints of law. Such a people are not likely to keep their eyes steadily upon the main chance like the Scotch or the Dutch. England strove very hard at one period to compel the Scotch to pay a double Church, but Sawney took his pen and ink, and finding what a sum it amounted to became furious and drew his sword. God forbid the Irishman should do the same! The remedy now would be worse than the disease; but if the oppressions of England had been more steadily resisted a century ago, Ireland would not have been the scene of poverty, misery, and distress which it now is.

The Catholic religion, among other causes, contributes to the backwardness and barbarism of Ireland. Its debasing superstition, childish ceremonies, and the profound submission to the priesthood which it teaches, all tend to darken men's minds, to impede the progress of knowledge and inquiry, and to prevent Ireland from becoming as free, as powerful, and as rich as the sister kingdom. Though sincere friends to Catholic emancipation, we are no advocates for the Catholic religion. We should be very glad to see a general conversion to Protestantism among the Irish, but we do not think that violence, privations, and incapacities, are the proper methods of making proselytes.

Such, then, is Ireland at this period—a land more barbarous than the rest of Europe, because it has been worse treated and more cruelly oppressed. Many of the incapacities and privations to which the Catholics were exposed have been removed by law, but in such instances they are still incapacitated and deprived by custom. Many cruel and oppressive laws are still enforced against them. A tenth part of the population engrosses all the honours of the country; the other nine pay a tenth of the product of the earth for the support of a religion in which they do not believe. There is little capital in the country. The great and rich men are called by business, or allured by pleasure, into England; their estates are given up to factors, and the utmost farthing of rent extorted from the poor, who, if they give up the land, cannot get employment in manufactures, or regular employment in husbandry. The common people use a sort of food so very cheap that they can rear families who cannot procure employment, and who have little more of the comforts of life than food. The Irish are light-minded— want of employment has made them idle; they are irritable and brave, have a keen remembrance of the past wrongs they have suffered, and the present wrongs they are suffering from England. The consequence of all this is, eternal riot and insurrection, a whole army of soldiers in time of profound peace, and general rebellion whenever England is busy with her other enemies or off her guard! And thus it will be, while the same causes continue to operate, for ages to come, and worse and worse as the rapidly increasing population of the Catholics becomes more and more numerous.

The remedies are time and justice, and that justice consists in repealing all laws which make any distinction between the two religions; in placing over the government of Ireland, not the stupid, amiable, and insignificant noblemen who have too often been sent there, but men who feel deeply the wrongs of Ireland, and who have an ardent wish to heal them; who will take care that Catholics, when eligible, shall be elected; who will share the patronage of Ireland proportionally among the two parties, and give to just and liberal laws the same vigour of execution which has hitherto been reserved only for decrees of tyranny, and the enactments of oppression. The injustice and hardship of supporting two Churches must be put out of sight, if it cannot or ought not to be cured. The political economist, the moralist, and the satirist, must combine to teach moderation and superintendence to the great Irish proprietors. Public talk and clamour may do something for the poor Irish, as it did for the slaves in the West Indies. Ireland will become more quiet under such treatment, and then more rich, more comfortable, and more civilised; and the horrid spectacle of folly and tyranny, which it at present exhibits, may in time be removed from the eyes of Europe.

There are two eminent Irishmen now in the House of Commons—Lord Castlereagh and Mr. Canning—who will subscribe to the justness of every syllable we have said upon this subject, and who have it in their power, by making it the condition of their remaining in office, to liberate their native country, and raise it to its just rank among the nations of the earth. Yet the Court buys them over, year after year, by the pomp and perquisites of office; and year after year they come into the House of Commons, feeling deeply, and describing powerfully, the injuries of five millions of their countrymen—and CONTINUE members of a government that inflicts those evils, under the pitiful delusion that it is not a Cabinet Question, as if the scratchings and quarrellings of Kings and Queens could alone cement politicians together in indissoluble unity, while the fate and torture of one-third of the empire might be complimented away from one minister to another, without the smallest breach in their Cabinet alliance. Politicians, at least honest politicians, should be very flexible and accommodating in little things, very rigid and inflexible in great things. And is this NOT a great thing? Who has painted it in finer and more commanding eloquence than Mr. Canning? Who has taken a more sensible and statesmanlike view of our miserable and cruel policy than Lord Castlereagh? You would think, to hear them, that the same planet could not contain them and the oppressors of their country—perhaps not the same solar system. Yet for money, claret, and patronage, they lend their countenance, assistance, and friendship to the Ministers who are the stern and inflexible enemies to the emancipation of Ireland!

Thank God that all is not profligacy and corruption in the history of that devoted people—and that the name of Irishman does not always carry with it the idea of the oppressor or the oppressed—the plunderer or the plundered—the tyrant or the slave! Great men hallow a whole people, and lift up all who live in their time. What Irishman does not feel proud that he has lived in the days of GRATTAN? who has not turned to him for comfort, from the false friends and open enemies of Ireland? who did not remember him in the days of its burnings and wastings and murders? No Government ever dismayed him—the world could not bribe him—he thought only of Ireland—lived for no other object—dedicated to her his beautiful fancy, his elegant wit, his manly courage, and all the splendour of his astonishing eloquence. He was so born and so gifted that poetry, forensic skill, elegant literature, and all the highest attainments of human genius were within his reach; but he thought the noblest occupation of a man was to make other men happy and free; and in that straight line he went on for fifty years, without one side-look, without one yielding thought, without one motive in his heart which he might not have laid open to the view of God and man. He is gone!— but there is not a single day of his honest life of which every good Irishman would not be more proud than of the whole political existence of his countrymen—the annual deserters and betrayers of their native land.

MOORE'S CAPTAIN ROCK.

*Memoirs of Captain Rock, the celebrated Irish Chieftain;
with some Account of his Ancestors.* Written by Himself.
Fourth Edition. 12mo. London, 1824.

This agreeable and witty book is generally supposed to
have been written by Mr. Thomas Moore, a gentleman of
small stature, but full of genius, and a steady friend of all
that is honourable and just. He has here borrowed the name
of a celebrated Irish leader, to typify that spirit of violence
and insurrection which is necessarily generated by systematic
oppression, and rudely avenges its crimes; and the picture he
has drawn of its prevalence in that unhappy country is at
once piteous and frightful. Its effect in exciting our horror
and indignation is in the long run increased, we think—
though at first it may seem counteracted—by the tone of
levity, and even jocularity, under which he has chosen to
veil the deep sarcasm and substantial terrors of his story. We
smile at first, and are amused, and wonder, as we proceed,
that the humorous narrative should produce conviction and
pity—shame, abhorrence, and despair.

England seems to have treated Ireland much in the same
way as Mrs. Brownrigg treated her apprentice—for which
Mrs. Brownrigg is hanged in the first volume of the Newgate
Calendar. Upon the whole, we think the apprentice is better

off than the Irishman; as Mrs. Brownrigg merely starves and beats her, without any attempt to prohibit her from going to any shop, or praying at any church her apprentice might select: and once or twice, if we remember rightly, Brownrigg appears to have felt some compassion. Not so Old England, who indulges rather in a steady baseness, uniform brutality, and unrelenting oppression.

Let us select from this entertaining little book a short history of dear Ireland, such as even some profligate idle member of the House of Commons, voting as his master bids him, may perchance throw his eye upon, and reflect for a moment upon the iniquity to which he lends his support.

For some centuries after the reign of Henry II., the Irish were killed like game, by persons qualified or unqualified. Whether dogs were used does not appear quite certain, though it is probable they were, spaniels as well as pointers; and that, after a regular point by Basto, well backed by Ponto and Caesar, Mr. O'Donnel or Mr. O'Leary bolted from the thicket, and were bagged by the English sportsman. With Henry II. came in tithes, to which, in all probability, about one million of lives may have been sacrificed in Ireland. In the reign of Edward I. the Irish who were settled near the English requested that the benefit of the English laws might be extended to them; but the remonstrance of the barons with the hesitating king was in substance this: "You have made us a present of these wild gentlemen, and we particularly request that no measures may be adopted to check us in that full range of tyranny and oppression in which we consider the value of such a gift to consist. You might as well give us sheep, and prevent us from shearing the wool, or roasting the meat." This reasoning prevailed, and the Irish were kept to their barbarism, and the barons preserved their dive stock.

"Read 'Orange faction' (says Captain Rock) here and you have the wisdom of our rulers, at the end of near six centuries, in statu quo. The grand periodic year of the stoics, at the close of which everything was to begin again, and the same events to be all reacted in the same order, is, on a miniature scale, represented in the history of the English Government in Ireland, every succeeding century being but a new revolution of the same follies, the same crimes, and the same turbulence that disgraced the former. But 'Vive l'ennemi!' say I: whoever may suffer by such measures, Captain Rock, at least, will prosper.

"And such was the result at the period of which I am speaking. The rejection of a petition, so humble and so reasonable, was followed, as a matter of course, by one of those daring rebellions into which the revenge of an insulted people naturally breaks forth. The M'Cartys, the O'Briens, and the other Macs and O's, who have been kept on the alert by similar causes ever since, flew to arms under the command of a chieftain of my family; and, as the proffered

HANDLE of the sword had been rejected, made their inexorable masters at least feel its EDGE."

Fifty years afterwards the same request was renewed and refused. Up again rose Mac and O, a JUST AND NECESSARY WAR ensued; and after the usual murders, the usual chains were replaced upon the Irishry. All Irishmen were excluded from every species of office. It was high treason to marry with the Irish blood, and highly penal to receive the Irish into religious houses. War was waged also against their Thomas Moores, Samuel Rogerses, and Walter Scotts, who went about the country harping and singing against English oppression. No such turbulent guests were to be received. The plan of making them poets-laureate, or converting them to loyalty by pensions of 100 pounds per annum, had not then been thought of. They debarred the Irish even from the pleasure of running away, and fixed them to the soil like negroes.

"I have thus selected," says the historian of Rock, "cursorily and at random, a few features of the reigns preceding the Reformation, in order to show what good use was made of those three or four hundred years in attaching the Irish people to their English governors; and by what a gentle course of alternatives they were prepared for the inoculation of a new religion, which was now about to be attempted upon them by the same skilful and friendly hands.

"Henry VII. appears to have been the first monarch to whom it occurred, that matters were not managed exactly as they ought in this part of his dominions; and we find him—with a simplicity which is still fresh and youthful among our rulers—expressing his SURPRISE that his subjects of this land should be so prone to faction and rebellion, and that so little advantage had been hitherto derived from the acquisitions of his predecessor, notwithstanding the fruitfulness and natural advantages of Ireland. Surprising, indeed, that a policy, such as we have been describing, should not have converted the whole country into a perfect Atlantis of happiness—should not have made it like the imaginary island of Sir Thomas More, where 'tota insula velut una familia est!'—most stubborn, truly, and ungrateful, must that people be, upon whom, up to the very hour in which I write, such a long and unvarying course of penal laws, confiscations, and Insurrection Acts has been tried, without making them in the least degree in love with their rulers.

"Heloise tells her tutor, Abelard, that the correction which he inflicted upon her only served to increase the ardour of her affection for him; but bayonets and hemp are no such 'amoris stimuli.' One more characteristic anecdote of those times and I have done. At the battle of Knocktow, in the reign of Henry VII., when that remarkable man, the Earl of Kildare, assisted by the great O'Neal and other Irish chiefs, gained a victory over Clanricard of Connaught, most important to the English Government, Lord Gormanstown, after the battle, in the first insolence of success, said, turning to the Earl of Kildare, 'We have now slaughtered our enemies, but, to complete the good deed, we must proceed yet further, and—cut the throats of those Irish of our own party!' Who can wonder that the Rock family were active in those times?"

Henry VIII. persisted in all these outrages, and aggravated them by insulting the prejudices of the people. England is almost the only country in the world (even at present) where there is not some favourite religious sport, where absurd lies, little bits of cloth, feathers, rusty nails, splinters, and other invaluable relics, are treasured up, and in defence of which the whole population are willing to turn out and perish as one man. Such was the shrine of St. Kieran, the whole treasures of which the satellites of that corpulent tyrant turned out into the street, pillaged the sacred church of Clonmacnoise, scattered the holy nonsense of the priests to the winds, and burnt the real and venerable crosier of St. Patrick, fresh from the silversmith's shop, and formed of the most costly materials. Modern princes change the uniform of regiments; Henry changed the religion of kingdoms, and was determined that the belief of the Irish should undergo a radical and Protestant conversion. With what success this attempt was made, the present state of Ireland is sufficient evidence.

"Be not dismayed," said Elizabeth, on hearing that O'Neal meditated some designs against her government; "tell my friends, if he arise, it will turn to their advantage— THERE WILL BE ESTATES FOR THOSE WHO WANT." Soon after this prophetic speech, Munster was destroyed by famine and the sword, and near 600,000 acres forfeited to the crown, and distributed among Englishmen. Sir Walter Raleigh (the virtuous and good) butchered the garrison of Limerick in cold blood, after Lord Deputy Gray had selected 700 to be hanged. There were, during the reign of Elizabeth, three invasions of Ireland by the Spaniards, produced principally by the absurd measures of this princess for the reformation of its religion. The Catholic clergy, in consequence of these measures, abandoned their cures, the churches fell to ruin, and the people were left without any means of instruction. Add to these circumstances the murder of M'Mahon, the imprisonment of O'Toole and O'Dogherty, and the kidnapping of O'Donnel—all truly Anglo-Hibernian proceedings. The execution of the laws was rendered detestable and intolerable by the queen's officers of justice. The spirit raised by these transactions, besides innumerable smaller insurrections gave rise to the great wars of Desmond and Hugh O'Neal; which, after they had worn out the ablest generals, discomfited the choicest troops, exhausted the treasure, and embarrassed the operations of Elizabeth, were terminated by the destruction of these two ancient families, and by the confiscation of more than half the territorial surface of the island. The last two years of O'Neal's wars cost Elizabeth 140,000 pounds per annum, though the whole revenue of England at that period fell considerably short of 500,000 pounds. Essex, after the destruction of Norris, led into Ireland an army of above 20,000 men, which was totally baffled and destroyed by Tyrone, within two years of their landing. Such was the importance of Irish rebellions two centuries before the time in which we live. Sir G. Carew attempted to assassinate the Lugan Earl—Mountjoy compelled the Irish rebels to massacre each other. In the course of a few months 3,000 men were starved to death in Tyrone. Sir Arthur Chichester, Sir Richard Manson, and other commanders, saw three children feeding on the flesh of their dead mother. Such were the golden days of good Queen Bess!

By the rebellions of Dogherty, in the reign of James I., six northern counties were confiscated, amounting to 500,000 acres. In the same manner, 64,000 acres were confiscated in Athlone. The whole of his confiscations amount to nearly a million acres; and if Leland means plantation acres, they constitute a twelfth of the whole kingdom according to Newenham, and a tenth according to Sir W. Petty. The most shocking and scandalous action in the reign of James, was his attack upon the whole property of the province of Connaught, which he would have effected, if he had not been bought off by a sum greater than he hoped to gain by his iniquity, besides the luxury of confiscation. The Irish, during the reign of James I., suffered under the DOUBLE evils of a licentious soldiery and a religious persecution.

Charles I. took a bribe of 120,000 pounds from his Irish subjects, to grant them what in those days were called Graces, but in these days would be denominated the Elements of Justice. The money was paid, but the graces were never granted. One of these graces was curious enough: "That the clergy were not to be permitted to keep henceforward any private prisons of their own, but delinquents were to be committed to the public jails." The idea of a rector, with his own private jail full of Dissenters, is the most ludicrous piece of tyranny we ever heard of. The troops in the beginning of Charles's reign were supported by the weekly fines levied upon the Catholics for non-attendance upon established worship. The Archbishop of Dublin went himself at the head of a file of musketeers, to disperse a Catholic congregation in Dublin—which object he effected after a considerable skirmish with the priests. "The favourite object" (says Dr. Leland, a Protestant clergyman, and dignitary of the Irish Church) "of the Irish Government and the English Parliament, was THE UTTER EXTERMINATION of all the Catholic inhabitants of Ireland." The great rebellion took place in this reign, and Ireland was one scene of blood and cruelty and confiscation.

Cromwell began his career in Ireland by massacring for five days the garrison of Drogheda, to whom quarter had been promised. Two millions and a half of acres were confiscated. Whole towns were put up in lots, and sold. The Catholics were banished from three- fourths of the kingdom, and confined to Connaught. After a certain day, every Catholic found out of Connaught was to be punished with death. Fleetwood complains peevishly "that the people DO NOT TRANSPORT READILY," but adds, "IT IS DOUBTLESS A WORK IN WHICH THE LORD WILL APPEAR." Ten thousand Irish were sent as recruits to the Spanish army.

"Such was Cromwell's way of settling the affairs of Ireland; and if a nation IS to be ruined, this method is, perhaps, as good as any. It is, at least, more humane than the slow, lingering process of exclusion, disappointment, and degradation, by which their hearts are worn out under more specious forms of tyranny; and that talent of despatch which Moliere attributes to one of his physicians is no ordinary merit in a practitioner like Cromwell: —"C'est un homme expeditif, qui aime a depecher ses malades; et quand on a mourir, cela se fait avec lui le plus vite du monde." A certain military Duke, who complains that Ireland is but half conquered, would, no doubt, upon an emergency, try his hand in the same line of practice, and, like that 'stern hero' Mirmillo, in the Dispensary,

"While others meanly take whole months to slay,
Despatch the grateful patient in a day!"

"Among other amiable enactments against the Catholics
at this period, the price of five pounds was set on the head of
a Romish priest, being exactly the same sum offered by the
same legislators for the head of a wolf. The Athenians, we
are told, encouraged the destruction of wolves by a similar
reward (five drachms); but it does not appear that these
heathens bought up the heads of priests at the same rate,
such zeal in the cause of religion being reserved for times of
Christianity and Protestantism."

Nothing can show more strongly the light in which the
Irish were held by Cromwell than the correspondence with
Henry Cromwell respecting the peopling of Jamaica from
Ireland. Secretary Thurloe sends to Henry, the Lord Deputy
in Ireland, to inform him that "a stock of Irish girls and Irish
young men are wanting for the peopling of Jamaica." The
answer of Henry Cromwell is as follows:- "Concerning the
supply of young men, although we must use force in taking
them up, YET IT BEING SO MUCH FOR THEIR OWN
GOOD, and likely to be of so great advantage to the public,
it is not the least doubted but that you may have such a
number of them as you may think fit to make use of on this
account.

"I shall not need repeat anything respecting the girls, not
doubting to answer your expectations to the full IN THAT;

and I think it might be of like advantage to your affairs there and ours here if you should think fit to send 1,500 or 2,000 boys to the place above mentioned. WE CAN WELL SPARE THEM; and who knows but that it may be the means of making them Englishmen—I mean, rather, Christians? As for the girls, I suppose you will make provisions of clothes, and other accommodations for them." Upon this, Thurloe informs Henry Cromwell that the council have voted 4,000 GIRLS, AND AS MANY BOYS, to go to Jamaica.

Every Catholic priest found in Ireland was hanged, and five pounds paid to the informer.

"About the years 1652 and 1653," says Colonel Lawrence, in his Interests of Ireland, "the plague and famine had so swept away whole counties, that a man might travel twenty or thirty miles and not see a living creature, either man, or beast, or bird, they being all dead, or had quitted those desolate places. Our soldiers would tell stories of the places where they saw smoke—it was so rare to see either smoke by day or fire or candle by night." In this manner did the Irish live and die under Cromwell, suffering by the sword, famine, pestilence, and persecution, beholding the confiscation of a kingdom and the banishment of a race. "So that there perished," says Sir W. Petty, "in the year 1641, 650,000 human beings, whose bloods somebody must atone for to God and the King!"

In the reign of Charles II., by the Act of Settlement, four millions and a half of acres were for ever taken from the Irish. "This country," says the Earl of Essex, Lord Lieutenant in 1675, "has been perpetually rent and torn since his Majesty's restoration. I can compare it to nothing better than the flinging the reward on the death of a deer among the pack of hounds, where every one pulls and tears where he can for himself." All wool grown in Ireland was, by Act of Parliament, compelled to be sold to England; and Irish cattle were excluded from England. The English, however, were pleased to accept 30,000 head of cattle, sent as a gift from Ireland to the sufferers in the great fire! and the first day of the Sessions, after this act of munificence, the Parliament passed fresh acts of exclusion against the productions of that country.

"Among the many anomalous situations in which the Irish have been placed, by those 'marriage vows, false as dicers' oaths,' which bind their country to England, the dilemma in which they found themselves at the Revolution was not the less perplexing or cruel. If they were loyal to the King de jure, they were hanged by the King de facto; and if they escaped with life from the King de facto, it was but to be plundered and proscribed by the King de jure afterwards.

"'Hac gener atque socer coeant mercede suorum.'— VIRGIL.

"'In a manner so summary, prompt, and high mettled,
Twixt father and son-in-law matters were settled.'

"In fact, most of the outlawries in Ireland were for
treason committed the very day on which the Prince and
Princess of Orange accepted the crown in the Banqueting-
house; though the news of this event could not possibly
have reached the other side of the Channel on the same day,
and the Lord-Lieutenant of King James, with an army to
enforce obedience, was at that time in actual possession of
the government, so little was common sense consulted, or
the mere decency of forms observed, by that rapacious spirit,
which nothing less than the confiscation of the whole island
could satisfy; and which having, in the reign of James I. and
at the Restoration, despoiled the natives of no less than ten
millions six hundred and thirty-six thousand eight hundred
and thirty-seven acres, now added to its plunder one million
sixty thousand seven hundred and ninety- two acres more,
being the amount altogether (according to Lord Clare's
calculation) of the whole superficial contents of the island!

"Thus, not only had ALL Ireland suffered confiscation
in the course of this century, but no inconsiderable portion
of it had been twice and even thrice confiscated. Well might
Lord Clare say, 'that the situation of the Irish nation, at
the Revolution, stands unparalleled in the history of the
inhabited world.'"

By the Articles of Limerick, the Irish were promised the free exercise of their religion; but from that period to the year 1788, every year produced some fresh penalty against that religion, some liberty was abridged, some right impaired, or some suffering increased. By acts in King William's reign, they were prevented from being solicitors. No Catholic was allowed to marry a Protestant; and any Catholic who sent a son to Catholic countries for education was to forfeit all his lands. In the reign of Queen Anne, any son of a Catholic who chose to turn Protestant got possession of the father's estate. No Papist was allowed to purchase freehold property, or to take a lease for more than thirty years. If a Protestant dies intestate, the estate is to go to the next PROTESTANT heir, though all to the tenth generation should be Catholic. In the same manner, if a Catholic dies intestate, his estate is to go to the next Protestant. No Papist is to dwell in Limerick or Galway. No Papist is to take an annuity for life. The widow of a Papist turning Protestant to have a portion of the chattels of deceased in spite of any will. Every Papist teaching schools to be presented as a regular Popish convict. Prices of catching Catholic priests, from 50s. to 10 pounds, according to rank. Papists are to answer all questions respecting other Papists, or to be committed to jail for twelve months. No trust to be undertaken for Papists. No Papist to be on Grand Juries. Some notion may be formed of the spirit of those times, from an order of the House of

Commons, "that the Sergeant-at-Arms should take into custody all Papists that should presume to come into THE GALLERY!" (Commons' Journal, vol. iii., fol. 976.) During this reign the English Parliament legislated as absolutely for Ireland as they do now for Rutlandshire, an evil not to be complained of, if they had done it as justly. In the reign of George I., the horses of Papists were seized for the militia, and rode by Protestants; towards which the Catholics paid double, and were compelled to find Protestant substitutes. They were prohibited from voting at vestries, or being high or petty constables. An act of the English Parliament in this reign opens as follows: —"Whereas attempts have been lately made to shake off the subjection of Ireland to the Imperial Crown of these realms, be it enacted," etc. etc. In the reign of George II. four- sixths of the population were cut off from the right of voting at elections by the necessity under which they were placed of taking the oath of supremacy. Barristers and solicitors marrying Catholics are exposed to all the penalties of Catholics. Persons robbed by privateers during a war with a Catholic State are to be indemnified by a levy on the Catholic inhabitants of the neighbourhood. All marriages between Catholics and Protestants are annulled. All Popish priests celebrating them are to be hanged. "This system" (says Arthur Young) "has no other tendency than that of driving out of the kingdom all the personal wealth of the Catholics, and extinguishing their industry within it;

and the face of the country, every object which presents itself to travellers, tells him how effectually this has been done."— Young's Tour in Ireland, vol. ii., p. 48.

Such is the history of Ireland—for we are now at our own times; and the only remaining question is, whether the system of improvement and conciliation begun in the reign of George III. shall be pursued, and the remaining incapacities of the Catholics removed, or all these concessions be made insignificant by an adherence to that spirit of proscription which they professed to abolish? Looking to the sense and reason of the thing, and to the ordinary working of humanity and justice, when assisted, as they are here, by self- interest and worldly policy, it might seem absurd to doubt of the result. But looking to the facts and the persons by which we are now surrounded, we are constrained to say that we greatly fear that these incapacities never will be removed till they are removed by fear. What else, indeed, can we expect when we see them opposed by such enlightened men as Mr. Peel—faintly assisted by men of such admirable genius as Mr. Canning—when Royal Dukes consider it as a compliment to the memory of their father to continue this miserable system of bigotry and exclusion, when men act ignominiously and contemptibly on this question, who do so on no other question, when almost the only persons zealously opposed to this general baseness and fatuity are a few Whigs and Reviewers, or here and there a virtuous poet like Mr. Moore? We repeat again, that the measure never will be effected but by fear. In the midst of one of our just and necessary wars, the Irish Catholics will compel this country to grant them a great deal more than they at present require or even contemplate. We regret most severely the protraction of the disease, and the danger of the remedy; but in this way it is that human affairs are carried on!

We are sorry we have nothing for which to praise Administration on the subject of the Catholic question, but it is but justice to say, that they have been very zealous and active in detecting fiscal abuses in Ireland, in improving mercantile regulations, and in detecting Irish jobs. The commission on which Mr. Wallace presided has been of the greatest possible utility, and does infinite credit to the Government. The name of Mr. Wallace in any commission has now become a pledge to the public that there is a real intention to investigate and correct abuse. He stands in the singular predicament of being equally trusted by the rulers and the ruled. It is a new era in Government when such men are called into action; and if there were not proclaimed and fatal limits to that ministerial liberality, which, so far as it goes, we welcome without a grudge and praise without a sneer, we might yet hope that, for the sake of mere consistency, they might be led to falsify our forebodings. But alas! there are motives more immediate, and therefore irresistible; and the time is not yet come when it will be believed easier to govern Ireland by the love of the many than by the power of the few, when the paltry and dangerous machinery of bigoted faction and prostituted patronage may be dispensed with, and the vessel of the State be propelled by the natural current of popular interests and the breath of popular applause. In the meantime, we cannot resist the temptation of gracing our conclusion with the following beautiful passage, in which the author alludes to the hopes that were raised at another great era of partial concession and liberality, that of the revolution of 1782, when, also, benefits were conferred which proved abortive because they were incomplete, and balm poured into the wound, where the envenomed shaft was yet left to rankle.

"And here," says the gallant Captain Rock, "as the free confession of weakness constitutes the chief charm and use of biography, I will candidly own that the dawn of prosperity and concord which I now saw breaking over the fortunes of my country, so dazzled and deceived my youthful eyes, and so unsettled every hereditary notion of what I owed to my name and family, that—shall I confess it—I even hailed with pleasure the prospects of peace and freedom that seemed opening around me; nay, was ready, in the boyish enthusiasm of the moment, to sacrifice all my own personal interest in all future riots and rebellions to the one bright, seducing object of my country's liberty and repose.

"When I contemplated such a man as the venerable Charlemont, whose nobility was to the people like a fort over a valley, elevated above them solely for their defence; who introduced the polish of the courtier into the camp of the freeman, and served his country with all that pure Platonic devotion which a true knight in the time of chivalry proffered to his mistress; when I listened to the eloquence of Grattan, the very music of freedom, her first fresh matin song, after a long night of slavery, degradation, and sorrow; when I saw the bright offerings which he brought to the shrine of his country— wisdom, genius, courage, and patience, invigorated and embellished by all those social and domestic virtues, without which the loftiest talents stand isolated in the moral waste around them, like the pillars of Palmyra towering in a wilderness!—when I reflected on all this, it not only disheartened me for the mission of discord which I had undertaken, but made me secretly hope that it might be rendered unnecessary; and that a country which could produce such men and achieve such a revolution, might yet—in spite of the joint efforts of the Government and my family—take her rank in the scale of nations, and be happy!

"My father, however, who saw the momentary dazzle by which I was affected, soon drew me out of this false light of hope in which I lay basking, and set the truth before me in a way but too convincing and ominous. 'Be not deceived, boy,' he would say, 'by the fallacious appearances before you. Eminently great and good as is the man to whom Ireland owes this short era of glory, OUR work, believe me, will last longer than his. We have a power on our side that "will not willingly let us die;" and, long after Grattan shall have disappeared from earth like that arrow shot into the clouds by Alcestes, effecting nothing, but leaving a long train of light behind him, the family of the ROCKS will continue to flourish in all their native glory, upheld by the ever-watchful care of the Legislature, and fostered by that "nursing-mother of Liberty," the Church.'"